The Unruly PhD

THE UNRULY PHD

DOUBTS, DETOURS, DEPARTURES, AND OTHER SUCCESS STORIES

REBECCA PEABODY

palgrave
macmillan

First published in 2014 by
PALGRAVE MACMILLAN®
in the United States—a division of St. Martin's Press LLC,
175 Fifth Avenue, New York, NY 10010.

Where this book is distributed in the UK, Europe and the rest of the world,
this is by Palgrave Macmillan, a division of Macmillan Publishers Limited,
registered in England, company number 785998, of Houndmills,
Basingstoke, Hampshire RG21 6XS.

Palgrave Macmillan is the global academic imprint of the above companies
and has companies and representatives throughout the world.

Palgrave® and Macmillan® are registered trademarks in the United States,
the United Kingdom, Europe and other countries.

ISBN: 978–1–137–37310–6

Library of Congress Cataloging-in-Publication Data

Peabody, Rebecca.
   The unruly PhD : doubts, detours, departures, and other success
stories / by Rebecca Peabody.
      pages cm
   Includes index.
   ISBN 978–1–137–37310–6 (paperback)
      1. Doctor of philosophy degree. 2. Doctoral students—Interviews.
   3. Doctoral students—Attitudes. I. Title.

LB2386.P43 2014
378.2—dc23   2014005089

A catalogue record of the book is available from the British Library.

Design by Newgen Knowledge Works (P) Ltd., Chennai, India.

First edition: August 2014

Contents

Part III   PhDs Redirected

Acknowledgments

To everyone who shared their stories with me, and to Sam, who always listens to mine.

Introduction

This is not a book about whether you should, or should not, go to graduate school; neither is it a how-to guide for surviving the experience—at least not in the traditional sense. It is, instead, a collection of first-person stories from real people—all with unique, unpredictable, sometimes messy lives—who are happily and successfully on the other side of a PhD, and willing to speak frankly about the challenges and decisions they faced along the way. It presumes a readership that is already convinced of the value of a PhD, and is interested in learning how others have navigated this complicated, rewarding experience, and to what uses—academic and otherwise—graduate education is being put.

An unruly PhD is one that defies expectations, but not necessarily on purpose. It diverges—sometimes wildly—from the orderly progression of academic accomplishments presupposed by programs and funding agencies. Life gets in the way. Earning a living doesn't leave enough time for research, or maybe other opportunities beckon. Partners and children take priority. The dissertation topic goes stale, or is scooped, or vetoed by advisors. A short break turns into months or years—or becomes permanent. Things feel out of control, and the challenge of finishing takes on mythological proportions, while the pressure to make it all count for something mounts. It's impossible—it can't be done! But it can't go on—it's got to end! And then it's over, one way or another, and looking back, you can't imagine it any other way. The mistakes and shortcomings and doubts somehow got you to the place you never knew you wanted to be. *The Unruly PhD* demonstrates that you can break the rules on your way to success; you can do it all wrong, and still get it right.

The stakes of earning a PhD have never been higher. Whenever the economy struggles, graduate school applications rise, as has been the case for the last several years. More people, with fewer opportunities elsewhere, are turning to graduate school. At the same time, the crisis in higher education continues—although, as many have pointed out, it can't really be considered a crisis anymore when it's been underway for so long. As universities rethink their priorities and structures, tenure-track positions—which were, and for many remain, the only worthwhile application of a PhD—are dwindling. As a result, more and more people are signing up for, and graduating with, PhDs while at the same time the number of permanent positions open to degree holders is in sharp decline. This state of affairs is far from new; however in recent years it has become increasingly urgent. From William Pannapacker's published warnings to potential applicants, to the explosion of blog posts reflecting on individual experiences of grad school, the "should you go" debate is intensely polemical, and reveals the personal, professional, and economic stakes of the decision.

For students who have already made a commitment to graduate education, this conversation may not be particularly helpful. But there are other resources. In response to the changing job market, a number of organizations and university-sponsored events now focus on broadening graduate students' professional horizons by discussing employment opportunities for PhDs beyond the tenure track. This is a positive—though recent—development, and it may take some time before these kinds of resources are widely available. In addition, there are numerous challenges that must be met before graduate students even reach the job-hunting stage. While programs vary from school to school, and between departments, some issues are relatively consistent. How do you keep up with a workload that can seem overwhelming? How do you invent and impose structure onto tasks that you may not fully understand? How do you maintain consistent goals, as well as the stamina to chip away at them, throughout a program that can last up to a decade? This is where the how-to books come in. There's a large and growing list that tackles questions about time management, breaking dissertations down into reasonably sized tasks, going on the job market—and beyond. They are, however, largely theoretical in tone and may exclude readers whose circumstances don't fit into the premises that underpin the strategy.

As a PhD student myself, I followed the "should you go" conversation, which was interesting and relevant, but of little use to me since I'd already gone—and was several years in. I consulted a few of the how-to books which made me feel like no problem was too big for the right productivity tool—until I returned to my own collection of moving targets and remembered that productivity required a clear, relatively stable goal. I found myself wanting—needing—a different kind of book. I wanted to read stories about people who had gone through the same things that I was going through, who had made it work one way or another, and who were willing to share the nontheoretical details with me. I wanted to have a beer with advanced graduate students who had nothing to lose by telling me their war stories. I wanted to read about people with circumstances and habits and predispositions that would singe the pages of the productivity books—yet who, nevertheless, made it through and on to some sort of bright future. I wanted what I suspected was missing from the CVs of the scholars I admired: the confusion, the shortcuts, the reboots, the existential crises.

I finally started to hear those stories after I'd finished and was on the other side—along with a critical mass of people from my grad school generation who had enough distance to feel comfortable talking about their experiences. As it turned out, everyone had war stories—and while they were fascinating and validating in turn, I realized how helpful they would have been a few years earlier. I don't think they would have led me to make different choices, but they would have helped me weather the difficult moments with considerably more equanimity and optimism for the future. I would have spent less energy on angst, and used it instead to put one of those productivity books to good use.

With that in mind, I set out to collect and document some of the stories I found inspiring. I talked with people I knew, with friends of friends, and as I shared my project with others, with people I met via recommendation. I flew around the country, drove to meet people in their offices, living rooms, or cigar bars, and called other countries to conduct interviews, then used the transcripts that resulted to craft first-person essays, or edited interviews, describing each person's graduate experience. The sidebars came together from the collective contributions of my extended grad school network. My interests are reflected not only in the selection of participants, but also in the organization of the essays and interviews; I want to know—and think readers will want to know—how each person came to graduate school: was it the culmination of a long-held dream, or a family's expectation, or was it more of a "why not" situation? What was the transition like—were there highlights, or hurdles? How did the experience conclude—and what came next, professionally? Personally?

The result—this collection of essays—came together organically, and reveals my own embeddedness in the humanities (most of the contributors are humanists as well) as well as the diversity of ways in which one can do a PhD. They also reveal several recurring themes. Feeling underprepared for the intensity of a PhD is common, and many people consider leaving at one point or another. Suspecting that one's own path through the PhD is uniquely divergent from the norm is nearly universal—so much so that idiosyncratic would seem to be the new normal. Families—partners, children, even parents—play a huge role in shaping the trajectory of a PhD, and in determining what kinds of opportunities are feasible afterward. Financial stability and access to health insurance have life-altering consequences. Nonacademic passions—surfing, music, art—are often put on hold for the duration of a PhD, only to take on renewed importance, sometimes even greater than that held by academia, afterward. Life does exist both within, and beyond, the ivory tower; the brass ring of tenure-track employment is the ultimate sign of success for some, but it is no shinier than the successful careers in writing, law, health care—and more—achieved by others.

The goals of this book are several. First, and foremost, this book speaks to students who are in the midst of the experience right now, who may be feeling isolated, anxious, underprepared, or overwhelmed. Second, by juxtaposing a number of different stories, I hope to point out that certain challenging experiences are endemic to the structure of graduate school; they are institutional in nature, rather than individual. Third, these stories undermine the pervasive myth that anyone who's cut out to be a career academic will have all the right opportunities before them at just the right moment. In fact, struggles, challenges, and moments of doubt are the norm, not the exception. As a fourth goal, I hope that these stories demonstrate that success in broader terms—professional and intellectual fulfillment, physical and mental health, meaningful work/life balance—is not tied to the tenure track. There are, indeed, inspiring stories here from tenured, tenure-track, and up-and-coming junior scholars. However, they are balanced by stories from people who earned a PhD and then found their dream jobs in nonacademic lines of work, or in an expanded version of academia, and by stories from people who left their programs part way through when they realized that the PhD was no longer the right path—or the only path—to their professional callings.

What is it that makes personal stories so helpful? In part, it is the sense of community they create—a community that can be especially reassuring when one spends a significant part of one's adult life in a subculture that is often opaque, or just down-right incomprehensible, to outsiders. There's another aspect to it though, that might be referred to as the practical expansion of imaginative limits. Even the best imaginations have habits and blind spots that aren't always self-apparent; and sharing stories can introduce new ways of responding to challenges, or new directions in which to look for opportunities. What one is capable of imagining determines what one can create; as a result, expanding one's imaginative limits has real, practical, sometimes urgent value.

The real-world work done through imaginative exercise is not limited to graduate students. I remember trying to explain graduate school culture to my parents who were very supportive, but too far removed from my rather unique environment to really grasp the pressures, or the stakes. That changed when my mother read a novel written by a young woman who attended a PhD program that was quite similar to my own, and that described its cultural environment in vivid detail. I still remember her calling me after she'd finished the novel to say "I get it now; I really get it." And she did. In that spirit, and as a final goal for this book, I hope that it finds its way beyond the most immediate audience—current, future, and past graduate students—to the hands of their friends and families who may gain further insight into the complexities of this unique and rewarding experience, and into the lives of their loved ones.

The stories that follow are divided into three parts. The first part focuses on people who completed PhDs and have, or are striving for, positions in tenure-track academia. The second part shifts attention to people who finished the PhD, then went on to work in nonacademic settings. Stories in the third part come from people who started a graduate program, then left when they realized that earning a PhD was no longer the right, or necessary, path to their chosen careers. Interviews with innovative thinkers who have, or who started, a PhD are scattered throughout the parts. The stories and interviews are personal, detailed, funny, heart-breaking, and inspiring; in short, they reveal how a diverse range of graduate students met challenges and made difficult decisions along the way to a variety of successful careers. They demonstrate that there are as many right ways to get through a PhD as there are students willing to forge their own paths.

Part I

PhDs in Academia

Chapter 1

Derek
PhD, Art History
Tenure-Track Assistant Professor

This academic path was not even acknowledged where I went to grad school. But it all worked out. Everything I did that I shouldn't have done, that they told me not to do, it all actually led to me being successful on the job market.

Getting There

Los Angeles has always been a part of who I am. The city, the coast, the surfing; I can't imagine living anywhere else. Academia is also a big part of my identity, but I didn't realize that until later on in life. My father was a university professor in the social sciences before he went to law school, so by the time I was born, he was both a lawyer and a professor. As a kid I was always on a college campus. I went to college in LA—the same school my parents had both attended—but I got there on a sports scholarship, not through academics. Up until my sophomore year, I thought I was going to be a professional water polo player. Back then, when I thought about my future, which I didn't do very often, I imagined a continuation of my sports-centric life. I was happy doing what I was doing: going to workouts twice a day, being a student–athlete. Everything changed when I hurt my shoulder during lifeguard training. At the beginning of my sophomore season I had to stop playing.

With water polo gone, I needed to focus my energies somewhere else and I got very into studying; I'd been doing well in my art history classes, so I declared an art history major. Eventually, it was time to graduate and my dream—playing professional water polo—was long gone. By then my father was working as an attorney, and I knew I didn't want to do what he was doing. My brother also went to law school and he was miserable. I knew that I didn't want to do what my then-girlfriend, now wife, was doing—she was a graphic artist with an entry-level job at a magazine where she worked really long hours in a tiny cubicle, which just seemed miserable. I wanted to stay on a college campus because that was where I was most comfortable. I wanted to keep the freedom that I'd had as an undergrad. I wanted to go surfing in the morning, then go to the library, and just get lost in books.

I have really great parents who never put any pressure on me. When I was younger, my mom would sometimes ask my dad, "Is it okay that he's not reading his books?" My dad would say, "Well, he's reading the sports page. As long as he's reading something." I met my wife when I was 21 years old and a junior in college and it was one of those moments, I knew that this was the person that I was going to spend my life with, and so she also played a role in the decisions I was making. She always supported whatever I wanted to do, whether that meant going to grad school, or being a waiter and surfing all the time. All she asked was that we support ourselves, and for me to contribute a thousand dollars a month toward that goal.

In a way, my nominal contribution to our finances was great preparation for graduate school because for the six to ten years it takes to complete a PhD, you're in this strange liminal space where everyone else you know is climbing the ladder and making more money and having a career; meanwhile you're a perpetual student, living on fellowships and part-time stuff, not advancing financially at all.

After undergrad, and before the PhD, I did a Master's degree in art history. I'd only applied to local universities—both out of consideration for my partner's fledgling career, and out of naiveté about how to build academic credentials. The one I got into wasn't especially prestigious, but there was a great young art history professor there and I really wanted to work with her. I was bummed because the school wasn't on the coast, and it was an hour and a half drive from where my partner and I were living. Oddly enough though, that became a really important part of the experience because I ended up commuting to school with my advisor, a brilliant, unbelievable scholar and really caring mentor.

She was the first professor who took an interest in what I was doing. Of course, I didn't tell her that I was surfing all the time. But we talked about my projects, about her projects, and it was the first time that I understood what it meant to be a professor. I really got a sense of how to think about all kinds of issues: intellectual issues, professional issues. When it came time to apply to PhD programs her letters of recommendation really made a difference. I applied to schools all across the country, but ultimately chose a program in LA at the same school where I'd been an undergrad because there was a professor in the program whose scholarship had become very influential to how I thought about the discipline.

Arguably, I'd already deviated from the path you're supposed to take if you're seriously committed to an academic career, but this was one of the first times that I knowingly broke the rules. Everyone at my Master's school told me I shouldn't get my PhD from the same school where I'd been an undergrad. They told me that it would look bad when I went on the job market; it would show a lack of exposure to the forces of art history, and it would indicate that I was very narrow in my focus. Now that I think about it, I am pretty narrow in my focus. They were right, but I decided to do it anyway because it was best for my wife, and it was a very comfortable choice for me. Everything important to us was already in the same city—both of our families, my lifeguarding job, a great professor that I really wanted to work with. Also, I was already thinking that maybe, in spite of conventional wisdom, building a network here might make it easier to get a job in LA when I went on the market, however many years later. I was already thinking, "How can I set myself up to not have to leave?" More rule-breaking, of course, because that's exactly what everyone says *not* to do. They all say "No, no, no; you're a failure unless you take the best possible job at the best possible institution, wherever that requires you to move." I won't say that all that advice coming from experts didn't make me nervous, but I was already planning to stay in LA.

Getting Through

I started graduate school for the second time, this time as a PhD student, and I loved it every bit as much as I thought I would. Those early years of graduate school were some of the happiest times of my life. I'd wake up early, go surfing, head to campus, go home for a bit, and then spend the rest of the day in the library. At the same time, my wife was changing careers—moving from being a graphic designer to working in the entertainment industry for a company that was really taking off. Her salary went up and that was great, but it also affected my view of where I was going to end up building a career. Am I going to take a job in rural Virginia for $35,000 a year and commute on the weekends to see my wife? Or seriously ask her to walk away from her job, which was already paying way more than I'd make as an assistant professor? My wife always said she'd do it; she said, "This is my time, professionally; when you graduate and get a job it'll be your time. We'll just pack everything up and go." Maybe she said that because she knew I could never live in rural Virginia. She's pretty smart.

When I got to graduate school, I found out that I was quite naïve about art history. I was a good writer and I got good grades, but in terms of being an original thinker, I wasn't very sophisticated. While I was taking my qualifying exams I felt a lot of academic pettiness and passive aggression from some of the faculty. They were critical of my perspective, and of my methodology—but it was never really clear whether the problem was me, or whether it was more about upper-level politics between the various professors.

My wife would want to hear about what I did during the day, but it's hard to explain the backstabbing, or the insecurity, to someone who's not living that experience. I was never really immersed in the grad student experience like some people are, which was both good and bad. On the one hand, at the end of the day I could treat it like a job—go home, have dinner with my wife, and talk about movies. But on the other hand, being able to check out each day didn't erase the tensions of grad school. The whole time my wife had to remind me: "No, no, no, you're going to finish your PhD; this is something you can do." I'd have moments of insecurity, and I'd be depressed and wonder what the hell I was doing. Was my dissertation topic even worth writing on? Why was I trying to translate some article from German into English? Sometimes it all seemed so stupid. There were definitely some dark moments where I thought "I'm not going to finish. I can't, I won't, and I don't even know why I'm here."

I hated the pettiness of it all; I hated the fact that it moved so slowly. I hated that one of my advisors made me feel stupid. You know, there are those moments where you're sitting in a seminar and there's someone who's just smarter than you and more perceptive in their analysis of texts and they have a lot of really interesting things to say. You're sitting there going "Shit! That's a really good point. I wouldn't have thought of that in a hundred years!" There were a lot of those kinds of people at my grad school. My entire life I've always felt a little bit—not stupid, but . . . I got into college through athletics, right? So, I've always been a bit insecure about that. There have always been smarter kids than me. Then, you get to graduate school and you're surrounded by the smartest kids. Every graduate student probably looks across the table and thinks "That person's really smarter than I am." I certainly did, and that brought on a lot of insecurity.

But, throughout the whole process I was thinking that if I didn't finish, if I didn't get a job, I'd just figure something else out. I'm good at cultivating an attitude of, "Oh well; I'll see how long I can ride this wave." I don't like corny surfing metaphors but the ocean can teach you a lot of lessons. There could be days when it looks calm and then you go out and have a near-death experience. There were times when I was rescuing people and the last thought in my mind was "Shit. I am going to die." That puts things in perspective.

Of course, surfing had to be kept secret the whole time I was in grad school because I didn't want to be typecast as a dumb surfer. Also, none of the other graduate students and professors seemed to have any hobbies outside of their work. They were all type A personalities: hard-working, committed to their jobs, no life outside of academia. I didn't want to be like that. I was also hiding the fact that my marriage was always going to be more important than graduate school. If I had to choose between making sure I had a healthy relationship with my wife, or writing the best one-page response paper to Derrida for tomorrow's seminar, Derrida was going to slide. Who knows how much posturing goes on in grad school, but it seemed like I was the only one prioritizing family. Every other grad student was reading nonstop, constantly in the library, and completely committed to the academic life. Meanwhile, I was caking on sunscreen and wearing hats while lifeguarding. I didn't want to have too much of a tan, or look like I was really physically active, because that's not how graduate students look.

After I advanced to candidacy, my wife and I decided to have a child. By that time I was writing my dissertation and adjunct teaching at a local liberal arts college. I was thinking that if I did a really great job, they might remember me later when openings came along. Our plan was that our daughter would be born, my wife would have four months of maternity leave, then she'd go back to work and I'd take care of our daughter during the day and write and teach my class at night. Of course, that was impossible because having a child is all-encompassing. When my wife went back to work I basically took a year off—I didn't do any work on my dissertation. Sometimes I'd go to the library planning to work and I'd end up playing solitaire because I just needed that space. Being with a baby all day long, and being the primary care-giver, is a really intense experience. It was just the two of us all day long—I was changing diapers, feeding her, getting her to go to sleep. It was a very lonely, very solitary, but fabulous experience. The first time she rolled over, I was there. Every word, I was the person who was there.

When my daughter was two, she started going to daycare two days a week which freed me up a bit—but leaving her for the first time was harrowing. I'd planned to drop her off and then come onto campus to prep for a lecture, but she cried so much; she didn't want me to leave and it was just awful. I finally left her, but by then I was a mess. I couldn't go to the library—I couldn't do anything. I had to go sit in the car and cry, then try to pull myself together to go teach my lecture. Not only were there times where I was crying before walking into a classroom, there were times when I was lecturing about modern and contemporary art with the theme of Teletubbies going through my head. Seriously, those first two years I watched Teletubbies every day and that's mind-numbing stuff. I'd find myself talking about Piet Mondrian and theosophy and in the back of my mind I'm actually thinking "Theosophy is like this utopian world, sort of like the Teletubby world. It's just free and easy, it's beyond language. It's universal—like Shangri La; theosophy and Teletubbies."

Throughout that process I was really sensitive about how people perceived me. I hated it when people called me Mr. Mom—suggesting that I'm not as much of a man because I'm not making the money for the family, or because I'm playing a role traditionally held by a woman. But it didn't make me bitter, just more sensitive. I see, hear, and read things differently now because of that experience and I think it makes me a better teacher and art historian.

There was a tipping point when my daughter was four and started going to school five days a week. For the first time, I had blocks of time to myself and I started to find that space I'd had before she was born. But those four years before she went to school were four years added on to my PhD that we hadn't expected. I hadn't planned on not writing a single page for a year. It just happened that way. It was absolutely terrifying at the time. It's a lot easier looking back on it than it was going through it.

Those years were tough for me in terms of my professional identity, and even though I wasn't working on my dissertation, I loved coming to campus one night a week, giving my three-hour lecture, then going home and grading papers. I started to get into the groove of teaching and I was doing well at it—getting asked back, and getting a lot of positive feedback. While I was adjuncting, the modern and contemporary art professor left, and I was hired as a temporary replacement. That meant full-time work with benefits, but a 4/4 teaching load—four classes per semester—which is intense. At that point I was nowhere near finishing my dissertation; I'd only written a chapter or two, and I was still the primary care-giver for our daughter. I'd pretty much stopped surfing and was in survival mode. It was so much work; it was awful, but it was great too. For the first time I had an office and a phone, and voice mail. I had a nametag on the door, and I got to go to faculty meetings. I had an identity, and a purpose. After eight years of graduate school you're just happy to get out of that liminal phase, even if you aren't really out.

Meanwhile, people from my cohort were applying for fellowships, TA'ing, and publishing. They were setting themselves up in a different way than I was setting myself up. My grad school was a research university and at places like that, they don't want their grad students teaching at liberal arts colleges. They want you to focus primarily on your scholarship, on publishing, and to get a job at another research university. I could barely find time to work on my dissertation—much less get publications out on the side. So, on the one hand, my peers were probably a little bit jealous that I already had a job, a salary, and a professional path even though I was still a grad student. But on the other hand, some of my professors just gave up on me, thinking, "Well, he's obviously a lost cause."

Putting my dissertation completely on hold while my daughter was young, then mostly on hold while I was teaching was really difficult, psychologically. Writing is already challenging; when you're trying to make time for it in a schedule that has no time to spare—well, I knew that I had to make a heroic effort or it would never get done. If you don't make the decision to be uncomfortable—sometimes extraordinarily uncomfortable—day after day, for years, it will never happen.

Somehow I did it, but not without a lot of politics and last-minute drama. I had five committee members, and by the time I was finishing, only one was still on campus. Two had left the country, one had moved to a different part of the state, and one had retired. The one still on campus was the one who had always been the most critical of what I was doing. She had other students who were progressing faster, publishing, doing what I should have been doing—instead, I was becoming that graduate student who took ten years to get his PhD. She didn't take me seriously. By the time I was ready to file I had a job offer, contingent on having my PhD in hand. I had everyone's signature except for this one advisor who'd given me up as a lost cause. She said, "Oh no, it's obvious that you need months, maybe even another year, to work on this." She was aggressively negative, and she would not sign off on the dissertation.

At that point, my life was in the balance. I had a job offer, and I was going to lose it if she didn't sign. It was only after other committee members put pressure on her that she reconsidered. Finally, the day before the last day to file, I got a call saying, "Oh, I didn't know I was the only one that didn't sign.

Of course I'll sign." Crisis averted, for the time being, but it's still a little bit awful when I think back. An experience like that doesn't just go away.

Moving On

My school opened up a tenure-track assistant professor search to replace the visiting professor spot that I was currently filling. I could see this amazing opportunity setting itself up—it was the ideal job, at the ideal school—a place I'd love to see myself building a career. Again, I'd broken a major rule. You're never supposed to adjunct at a place where you might apply for a tenure-track position, because they won't take you seriously; they'll always think of you as an adjunct. But I worked really hard, I taught 4/4, advised students, built relationships with the department and with the rest of the faculty—all the things a visiting professor's not supposed to do. And they acknowledged my hard work. When they wrote the tenure-track position, it was really focused on all the areas where I'm strongest. It emphasized the importance of teaching; it listed the classes that I'd already taught. I was the inside candidate, and I started getting nervous. I was like, "oh my god—could this really happen?" It was so exciting and so nerve-wracking at the same time. They were bringing in other candidates to interview, and I'm there in my office so I'm watching them walk down the hall past my door.

I had gone on the job market and had a series of campus interviews at other universities and that made me feel, for the first time, like I could compete on a national level. The places where I had interviews were liberal arts universities or master's granting institutions, and the fact that I had significant teaching experience beyond the TA level, that I'd finished my dissertation while working full time as an academic teaching a 4/4 course load—these were considered strengths, not weaknesses. In the interview, when they asked me, "How would you deal with a business major taking an introductory art history class?" I could say, "Oh, well I've had that experience and here's how I've dealt with it." Or when they'd ask, "How do you plan on fulfilling your publication goals while teaching at a 3/3 course load?" I could say, "I am currently teaching a 4/4 and I finished my dissertation." I didn't know these were areas of strength I was developing, because this academic path was not even acknowledged where I went to grad school. But it all worked out. Everything that I did that I shouldn't have done, that they told me not to do, actually led to me being successful on the job market.

I got an offer from a school in rural Virginia. It was beautiful; we could've owned a five acre house on a river, in the foothills of Appalachia. The whole time I was looking around, asking myself "Could I live here?" And, you know, no, I couldn't. But before I turned it down I came back to my school here, where I was still a candidate for the job I truly wanted—my dream job. I asked them, "What should I do?" And they said, "You need to wait because we have other candidates coming, but please wait." So I turned down a solid job offer in a really tight market, not because I had a better one—but because I wanted so badly for this other offer to come through. The gamble paid off; they offered me my dream job: tenure track, in the city where I grew up, where our families live, where my wife built her career. I'm a huge Dodgers fan, and I got to keep my season tickets. It's like; "Oh my god!" This never happens! Or that's what they say, anyway.

The last five years have been fabulous—I think I went through the more difficult period as a graduate student. My daughter is older, which makes things easier. I like my colleagues. I like my classes. I like the fact that I'm teaching, writing, editing, and curating shows. Finally, some things are paying off; I'm starting to get recognition for my work which is very gratifying.

I'm still the parent with the more flexible schedule, and my job is still the one that's considered less serious in some ways. I've cancelled class when my daughter's sick or has a doctor's appointment; if someone's going to miss work, it's going to be me. I understand why it has to be that way. My wife's job is corporate; she works in an industry that generates millions of dollars. People really depend upon her. I can cancel office hours for the week if I have to, but when she's in a meeting, she's *in a meeting*.

When it comes down to it, what I'm doing *is* more flexible. I may be the one who has to adjust, but I also have that freedom that I love. Every semester I cancel a class to go surfing. It's just one of those things I do. I learned this year that I should tell my wife first, because if she's looking for me, if she thinks I'm in the classroom and I'm not, it's not good. She doesn't realize that surfing is my mistress.

Chapter 2

Josephine
PhD, Classics
Adjunct Professor

It always comes back to this gut feeling that this is my passion, this is my path, and I shouldn't give up on it. I mean, it may not work out, but if it doesn't work out, it's not going to be because I gave up. That's the only thing I can do, right? . . . I never thought that getting a PhD in Classics was going to teach me to be present in the moment.

Getting There

I always knew that I wanted to teach. Even before I started college I had this weird feeling, like intuition or something, that I wanted to be a college professor. Honestly, I have no idea where it came from; I don't think I knew any college professors growing up, and I'm the first person in my family to go to college. I remember talking to my dad when I was around 12 years old and telling him that I wanted to be a professor; he said that I would never be able to do that because to be a professor you have to write a book. I remember thinking, and that's impossible...why? Why can't I write a book? Is that really such a big deal? I read them all the time! So I said, "Fine; I'll be a park ranger." He said, "Oh, those jobs are *highly* coveted and much harder to get than you would think." And I was like, "Oh, great."

Later on, I met this woman whose parents were smart, and liberal, but also quite poor, and they were helping her do research for colleges where she might go. They found this small, public, liberal arts school in the Northwest that sounded amazing. I ordered the catalog and read through it, and I was like, oh, my god; yes—it was interdisciplinary, with an incredible curriculum, just a wonderful school. So I went to visit her and to check out the school and the town, but it was really quite unnecessary. I knew I wanted to go there—there was not a doubt in my mind. I loved it. The Pacific Northwest is so beautiful, so dreary! I was trying to figure out my sexuality at the same time, and when I got there I found a considerable lesbian population—I saw lesbian couples out in the streets, hand in hand. I was like, yes!

I moved out there early so I could find a job, work for a year, and establish residency in order to lower tuition. At first I worked at a daycare, but then I got this amazing job providing support to people with developmental disabilities. It was incredible, and turned out to be so much more than a job—but it was also very much a job, and I was very busy all through school—working full time, and taking a full course load. I remember writing those tuition checks every quarter and sweating bullets just being like, dear god, why am I doing this? Please don't bounce. But I did it, and I loved it. I worked my butt off, at work and at school. I can see looking back that it would've been nice to have a little more time to socialize. My first relationship with a woman was really, really hard, because

I was so busy and so tired. But my feelings about school—and all the work that was necessary to pay for it—were really clear. I just knew; this was it for me. The intuitive pull toward being a professor was always there.

I graduated after a very successful college career, but I was confused about what to do next. Classics seemed like the field for me but I had only ever done Classics in translation as part of my interdisciplinary courses and I didn't have Greek and Latin, which are the basic building blocks of a degree in Classics. One of my professors put me in touch with a former graduate student who was doing a PhD in history. We met for coffee, and I told her that I would really love to learn Greek and do Classics. Then I told her about what I should do instead—like a psychology PhD, which I could have pretty much started right away. By that time I had all this experience with social work. The agency that I had been working for had offered me a full-time job building and supporting an educational program at the organization. That seemed like what I should do, and then I should probably do a psychology PhD in the evenings. And she was like, learn the Greek! It's so obvious that's where your heart lies. I'd been telling her, earlier, how important it was to me to feel like I was making some change in the world, making it better, impacting people in a positive way. She told me the best way to achieve that would be to do the thing that I was good at and most passionate about. That struck me as very true. So I did it. After working full time to pay for a four-year undergrad degree, I signed up to do it again; I went back to school and studied Greek and Latin. It took me four more years, and I earned a second BA.

By then, my current partner and I were together. We started dating when I was a junior in college—the first time through—so she's ridden this whole crazy wave with me. She was a little more tolerant of my super busy schedule, but she really did not understand why I was going back to school the second time around. She was not impressed at all. I'm not going to lie to you. At a certain point I had to do a lot of soul searching and basically say to her: I am doing this. I'm going to learn these languages however long it takes me. Could be two years, could be four years. I didn't know. Then I'm going to apply to graduate school, which means I'll be moving again. She was like, "This is awful." She hated the idea that what I was doing was just preparing to further destabilize us. But I explained it to her in no uncertain terms, and connected it back to this gut feeling I have that this is my passion, and my path, and that I shouldn't just give up on it, you know? I mean, it may not work out, but if it doesn't work out, it's not going to be because I gave up. That's the only thing I can do. Right? When I presented it to her that way, and showed her how important it was to me, she let me do it, and she has never questioned it since. If she had reacted otherwise I might have never done all of this.

The second BA served its purpose. I'd heard that undergraduates in Classics at my school could expect to get into one-third of the grad programs that they applied to, so I applied to 11, thinking it would be nice to have three or four choices. But I got into 10 of the 11—and almost half of them Ivies. It seems great, but it was actually quite overwhelming. At one point, after I got another acceptance letter, I accidentally e-mailed the administrator at an Ivy League school, something like, "Holy fucking shit, not another one." It was supposed to be a forward, but I hit reply and added my advisors, and sent it. I was using the little computer in my department, and I let out the longest stream of expletives ever. I guess we all have our nightmare e-mail story, right?

Ultimately, after visiting a couple of places together, I let my partner decide. She chose here; she totally felt it, right from the beginning. And that was actually really nice for me, because I was freaking out about how to make the decision, and then I didn't have to decide. That was sort of great. I was psyched. I was like, these are all amazing programs. I would be so lucky to go to any one of them, and if I can make it through the program with my partner, and we can still have a good relationship, that would be fucking awesome. So we did it.

Getting Through

I loved my program, but there were some big challenges. I have a lot of anxiety around exams, and Classics is a pretty exam-heavy PhD program. Clearly I'm not smart enough to have taken that into account when I chose my field! We had sight translation exams in Ancient Greek and Latin with no dictionary or any assistance at all. They aren't living languages—it's not like you can go live in Ancient Greece for three months to get really fluent, you just have to study your balls off. That's, like, my worst nightmare. The language thing was still hard for me, because I had only been doing it for four years, and some people had been doing Latin since middle school or high school. I love the languages, especially Greek, and that helped. The philosophy, the literature—I really felt it, but it is hard. I'm not going to lie. I was just reading some Greek earlier today and I was like, man, I'm too pregnant for this. I'm tired! I just want to knit. So I spent those first few years just completely freaked out. There's Greek translation, Latin translation, plus French or Italian and German; Roman History, Roman Literature and Culture, Greek History, Greek Literature and Culture. That's a lot of exams, and they're all very unforgiving. You sit down in a room. You have three hours. Go—clock's ticking. There was never a time when I wasn't preparing for an exam, and at the same time, taking seminars, writing papers, going to conferences, trying to keep up with everything else.

My partner hadn't yet moved to join me. She was wrapping up her job and dealing with some health issues—it was a really difficult time for her. But I was torn and part of me was angry, because I was like, you were the one that chose this city—we should have come here together. I didn't want to go first and start this thing all by myself. It was awful. My car got stolen, so then I had no car. I had no partner. I was just miserable. My first semester I had to go up to my professors and say, I'm not going to be here for a week and a half because my partner's having surgery. But that was actually one of the moments when I felt I had chosen the right place, because all my faculty were completely supportive; they were just so lovely about it. Then when she was able to join me, it wasn't an easy transition. She was part way through a master's degree and we thought she could complete the internship requirements here, but we were totally naïve: different states, different licensing systems; she would have had to start all over. So she'd left her job, only to find out that she couldn't complete the training necessary for the career she'd planned to pursue here. It was a rough time. We went to couples counseling. We almost split up. Eventually we made it through, and she realized that what she wanted to do next was start her own business focusing on landscaping and organic gardening.

Those were the biggest challenges in the early years; my anxiety about exams, and trying to be a supportive partner, while also doing something—i.e., grad school—that really doesn't structurally support the fact that students actually have lives, right? That they have partners who might have some needs, you know? In retrospect, my partner was doing something that was probably more significant than what I was doing. I mean, she actually started a business which is now thriving and is quite wonderful.

There were times when I thought about quitting, but I'd tell myself that entertaining that fantasy was just creating the scenario that I was afraid might happen. Quitting is a preemptive fail, unless you are quitting because you have discovered that you are on the wrong path. Besides, I never felt like the aspects that I disliked outweighed how gratifying it was to be so monumentally challenged. I was profoundly moved by the work that I was doing. I was reading Sappho in Greek after I was finally good enough to do it, and I was comfortable and confident enough with who I was as a person that I was okay with the fact that she's famous for being a lesbian. To bring those things together, to say this is my life and that's okay, and just sit down and read it in Greek, I would just cry. Plus, Greek poetry is incredibly beautiful. You know, when you study meter, and you see how a poet like Sappho or Homer puts their pieces together so that the form and the meaning combine, and then you see traces of that throughout literature and philosophy...The experience was really, exactly, what I wanted it to be.

Part of what helped me adjust to graduate school was creating boundaries around it so that I didn't feel like I had to work all the time. Boundaries helped me deny that pressure, or reject it, and not allow it to be true for me. I had to learn how to say I'm not going to quit, but I *am* going to set some boundaries, and if setting those boundaries causes me to fail, then that's a litmus test—and this is not the career for me. I just couldn't go on, year after year, in the same way I'd lived through the first few years of grad school.

So when I got to the dissertation, I set some boundaries— and one of them was working at a library. I moved my desk out of my house, so I no longer had the option of constantly working, and got set up in a carrel. I left my dissertation at the library every day—I didn't bring it home. I worked some pretty long hours for sure but I always took Sundays off. Maybe, once in a while, if my committee was waiting for something or I was feeling extra crazy I'd work a Sunday afternoon but it was hard because I didn't have a desk at home anymore. I commuted to the library with a woman who worked four ten-hour days. She didn't work on Fridays, so I'd stay home on Fridays and catch up on reading. But then I'd always go on Saturdays for a long day. So I was doing more, maybe, than a 40-hour work week, but not more than what a lot of people do for their jobs. I would go for jogs in the evening, and take long walks with my partner. Sometimes I would take a day or two off and help her when she was really busy with her business.

Anxiety is so irrational. The dissertation was actually much more difficult than any of those exams, but it just wasn't as scary to me. I didn't feel like having one bad day could be a deal breaker the way it could if it just happened to fall on exam day. Maybe, also, it's because I worked full time through undergrad. I know how to do the long haul, I know how to work the long hours, I know how to push through. The dissertation wasn't as scary to me because I had a fellowship year and writing was my full-time job, whereas I was used to juggling full-time school, plus full-time work that wasn't even related to school. So only having one job? I mean it was a little monotonous actually but it was also the reward, you know? To get to do my own work was the prize at the end.

It took me seven and a half years—start to finish. I was supposed to be done in five years, but my department was really flexible and I never felt bullied or pressured. I wasn't even done with my exams and prospectus until four and a half years in. Because of my anxiety about the exams, I pushed them back as far as I could so I had time to over-prepare; looking back it's like I just tortured myself for four years instead of three. Plus I kept volunteering to teach, which extended things. I had funding from the department, and then from teaching. When there wasn't any teaching available, I worked for my partner. Everything worked out well at the end. My dissertation's a little wacky, as you would expect coming from me. But my committee was actually really impressed with it. They said that, compared with others they'd seen, it was extremely innovative. They could tell I'd done a lot of new work, which is rare, actually, in dissertation research where there's pressure to add something new but small to an already well-established research paradigm. Mine has a whole different methodological approach. I should really get off my ass and try to publish something from it.

Moving On

There's nothing like a PhD program—the goal is actually to work yourself out of your own job; that's what you do. Success is no longer being a grad student, and therefore, no longer being employable in the grad school industry. The goal is to dis-employ yourself. That's a tough one for me. In some ways I'm quite practical; I've always had jobs, I've always worked hard, I've never been unemployed before, and it's not at all appealing. Psychologically, finishing the dissertation was a little odd for that reason. Like I said, my department didn't put that much pressure on me and a part of me was like, why am I even finishing? I should just stay in graduate school forever. I was getting pretty good at it.

After I graduated I got an adjunct position teaching one class at a small liberal arts college here in town. I loved it, but it was also bittersweet because, honestly, it was pretty close to my dream job—but, of course, it was temporary. I had been on the market twice by then, once before I finished and once after and I had interviews both times, but I never made it past that stage. I suppose that was part of the melancholy of it all. Part of me was nervous about getting a job that would mean leaving this town we love, along with my partner's business, and so that made the adjunct position even more almost perfect; it was local and if it could have been an actual, full-time, tenure-track job...Well, it'd just be such a dream. The worst thing for me about contract work is not being able to become a part of the community. So that was hard, you know; one class, one day a week. I felt very peripheral, except in the classroom where everything was going really well.

Every Wednesday on my way home, I would be so high on the experience of teaching and being with the students; I loved giving them their workshops and hearing what they had to say, watching them learn and learning from them. After a few weeks, I remember saying to a friend that if this class is the only class I ever teach as faculty, that's okay. I still did it, you know, I passed the exams, I wrote a dissertation, I got a PhD, I taught a class on gender in ancient Greece at a small liberal arts college and it was successful and the students thrived and I learned a lot. I did it; that's my dream, that's what I wanted to do.

I never thought that getting a PhD in Classics was going to teach me to be present in the moment. I didn't think that was the lesson that I was doing all of this to learn. One of the things that Buddhist monks do is clean their temples. Maybe they're doing it, in part, so that the temple will be clean, but it's also a way to be present in the moment. All you're doing is scrubbing your little spots and being very focused on the task at hand. That's sort of what I feel like I'm doing; I'm just cleaning the temple. I have another adjunct position now at a different university, and if I think about it in terms of my day-to-day, it's still my dream job. I go to school and I have an office that I'm using, which is lovely. It's really fun to have space, even if it's not permanent. It's mine and it has my name outside the door.

So I go to my office and I reread the material before class, I write the workshops, I think about what my aims are for the day, how they fit in with my objectives for the week, and how they fit in with the arc of the course over the semester. I get to read a book for a speaker that's coming later in the week and I read that book like I'm cleaning the temple. I don't know that reading that book, or having a conversation with the visiting speaker is going to do shit for me in my career, but I don't think about it that way, you know? Okay, so is that professional networking? Yeah, sure. But I don't think that way because that doesn't work for me. I just do it the way that works for me, which is to say... nobody's life is perfect, but I am doing the things that I'm passionate about as best as I can in the circumstances that I have.

Some days are better than others; there's no doubt. Being a contract employee is hard, I can't deny it. I get anxious that I won't get another job. I don't have health insurance over the summer through my contract, so I really need to look at what our options are. There are days when I'm just like, ugh, I would trade it all for a job—just a job. I feel like some of the things that I really want, the things that I'm missing – like really putting down roots, like really building my community – those are things that I could do even if I got a job that I didn't love, that I just had for the sake of having a job. But then I look at the economy and I ask myself, what is this "job" that I could do that would have these awesome benefits and be really secure, and I wouldn't love it, but I wouldn't necessarily hate it of course, and somehow I'd be qualified to do it? Then reality sets in. I'm not alone; and it's not like I'm underemployed just because I'm an academic. It is not a wonderland of easy employment options out there. I mean there are people who were laid off from long-term jobs who have been unemployed for years now, struggling... It's much bigger than me. So with that in mind, I figure, I do have the skill set, the training, and the credentials for this one particular job that is also the thing that I most want to do, so I probably shouldn't give up on it quite yet.

And I have big dreams, big plans. I have this proposal in mind for how to start a series of small colleges. They'd be integrated into their local communities, yet function as liberal arts schools, because I know from my own college experience that those two things are not mutually exclusive. They would be affordable, and they would provide an integrated education to a few thousand people a year, grant bachelor's degrees, and I would teach at one of those colleges and, like all the faculty, take my turn at administrative work. That way, I'd be able to stay here in this town that we love where I do have a very strong community and my partner has a thriving business. I would get to feel that I was really making a difference—that I was contributing something. I'd have my family. And a big organic garden.

Chapter 3

Jennifer
PhD, Art History
Postdoctoral Fellow

I think it would help people to hear more stories about what grad school life is like. People need to know, you're not crazy; it's not just you!

Getting There

Art was a big part of my life for a long time. I started out doing a lot of drawing and painting, and basically just exploring studio techniques. I was very committed to the *making* aspect of art making—creating objects that one could hang on a wall in a gallery or museum—and this practice continued into my undergraduate years, when I actually majored in studio art. What I found throughout those years was that I was much more interested in the research process that took place prior to the making of objects. For me, that process often involved reading texts that grappled with a lot of the issues that were of interest to me, whether they were about race, sociology, etc.

And I found that I was much more interested in the process of reading, looking, and writing about these issues than I was in translating my take on those issues into a material object. So by the time I had completed my senior thesis, in conjunction with completing a senior exhibition that was full of objects that I had made, I had realized that the thesis writing part of that requirement was just of more interest to me. I found it more compelling, and I wanted to extend that process into a dissertation-writing process, which can only be taken up within the context of graduate education.

I made the decision to go to grad school at the end of my senior year, which meant that if I applied in the fall, it would be another full year before I started. In the meantime, I thought I'd better find a way to keep in touch with the arts, while still making a living. My undergraduate advisor was incredibly supportive, always alerting me to new internship opportunities, and with her help I spent the year interning at a major gallery on the East Coast. I talked with a lot of people working at the gallery with me who were currently in the process of completing a PhD or had already completed their degree, and just asking them for their advice regarding the application process, and finding out about the challenges of graduate school. I'd also had several summer internships at museums on the West Coast during my undergraduate years, so that was another source of scholars who had PhDs in art history. I think talking with all those people helped me realize that earning a PhD was a possibility for me too, and kind of spurred my interest in the whole project.

I'm the only member of my family who's ever completed a PhD, so there were no prior examples closer to home. Our parents admonished my siblings and I to go to college, but after college it was just assumed that we would get jobs. However, I think being in contact with intellectuals, those who had decided to take on an area of specialization and research it to their hearts' content, opened a door for me, and I realized that a life of the mind was something that was possible, that could be funded, and that could eventually turn into a way of making a living.

I initially thought that I would come back to the West Coast and take up a PhD at one of the local schools in my home city, but others were advising me to look at the big schools with prestigious programs on the East Coast, because that would in some way broaden my horizons—put me in contact with important people in the field, etc. So that's what got me looking at schools on the East Coast. My goal was to work with scholars who were well known in the field of African-American art history, so I specifically looked at programs with scholars who had published on contemporary African-American art, which is my area of specialization. I only applied to four schools ultimately, and each of them had scholars who I thought were doing important work in my field. I was accepted at three out of the four, and pretty easily narrowed it down to two that I had to choose between. One offered more money, and I guess that made the choice a no-brainer. So I moved from the East Coast museum, back home to California for the summer, then back to the East Coast to start grad school in the fall.

Getting Through

The transition was, in a word, difficult—and for a variety of reasons. As an undergrad, I was heavily mentored and guided through my program by the professors in my department. It was a very warm, friendly, supportive department, and in many ways I was kind of coddled; I was one of a small number of students who were in my major. Up until that point, I hadn't encountered much competition between myself and my peers. We were all kind of going in our own directions work-wise; there was no conflict of interest. So the shift from that environment to a learning environment that was competitive was a big one; the students were no longer interested in sharing information or learning together like as a group of equals but, rather, in outshining others. Proving themselves to be the smartest person in the room, the most engaged person—the one with the most valuable ideas. Everyone received the same amount of funding, so I think competition got redirected toward other ends—toward being perceived as the best and brightest, or competing for the affections of the professors in the department. "I want to be so-and-so's favorite." That was a shock. Also, it was a bit of a shock to be perceived of as a producer of knowledge as opposed to a receiver of knowledge. In undergrad, you're applauded if you can read the assigned texts and regurgitate their essential points precisely and correctly. Within the context of graduate school, you're applauded when you can come up with a provable and substantive original idea, which was a difficult task for me, having been someone who was not as familiar with the discipline of art history as my peers were. So yeah, the transition was difficult for me at times in those initial years.

Part of what made it complicated was that I had studied studio art in college rather than art history. I didn't feel like I was on the same playing field as my peers. I felt that I had to work doubly hard to catch up, to rid myself of the knowledge deficit that I felt I was carrying around. So I read as much as possible, and more than my peers were reading, so that I wouldn't feel like an imposter of sorts, or unworthy of the degree that I was pursuing. It's funny—the Ivies are perceived of as being hypercompetitive and very demanding of their students, and they are, but I think so much of the pressure originates from the students themselves. There were times when my advisors tried to encourage me and my efforts and let me know that I was doing fine. But somehow I seldom ever believed them, and always felt that I should be doing better. So yeah, a lot of that pressure originates from the student.

But not all of it was internal. I do think a lot of that pressure was generated by my own lifelong perfectionism—which is ridiculous. But part of it was external, and I think some of that external pressure was race-based. I was the only African-American in my program at the time and I did feel that, for that reason, I was a very salient object in my environment, that I was somehow more visible, and therefore subject to more scrutiny by my peers and professors. I didn't feel that I could necessarily blend in. I felt that whenever I made a comment in a seminar, people were more alert and interested in assessing whether or not the comment proved or disproved that I was an affirmative action admit. So I think I felt both internal and external pressure to make it clear to everyone that I had earned my way into the program, and that I was ready to earn my keep. I wanted to perform in such a way that no one could think I was there for reasons other than those that were merit-based.

All of the pressure and the anxiety and the work around those early years took a toll on social relationships. In college I was pretty balanced. I had a very close group of friends, but I also took a lot of pride and pleasure in my work. I had my literature courses that required that I write papers, and I explored the city on the weekends with my friends; it was a pretty well-adjusted life. That can be attributed, in large part, to the fact that I didn't feel the pressure to prove myself. I think once you're weighed down in graduate school by the pressure to prove yourself, not just as a student but as an African-American student, your goal in life becomes turning into the absolute best in your respective field so as to kind of alleviate those pressures. So a lot of your time is just spent reading and rereading authors who are deemed important, and writing and rewriting papers, and your focus just narrows—socially and academically. A lot of social life—other interests, friendships, dating—kind of gets cut out or left by the wayside, all in the name of achieving this goal: proving yourself.

I think my parents were sympathetic to the struggles and challenges that I encountered. There were times when I would acknowledge some resentment or bitterness that I was feeling toward peers who I felt were giving me a hard time, and my parents might say, "That's small stuff; slough it off, ignore it, why pay any attention to that?" But I guess it's like, unless you're dealing with these difficult personalities yourself, you may not realize how challenging it can be to cope with trying to achieve a high-level performance in an environment that may be a bit hostile.

I had doubts about whether or not I would stay in the program throughout the course of my second year, and especially at the beginning of that year. They were triggered, in part, by an episode that had taken place within the context of a seminar where I got into a very heated discussion with a peer, and the peer acted in a manner that I perceived to be disrespectful. I think that episode triggered for me memories of previous instances where I had felt disrespected by hypercompetitive peers who'd say things like "I don't want to make you look bad," or whatever, before trying to do just that. I was deciding whether or not the hostility that those events were creating for me was something that I could continue to contend with throughout the course of the program. However, by the end of the second year my feeling was, okay I'm done with course work, I just need to knock out these generals and then I can get out of here. So by the time I was preparing for exams I had decided that I would continue on—with the understanding that once I completed my requirements I could leave, I could be based somewhere else for the research and the writing.

The exams went relatively well. I mean, you're given this huge bibliography of books and articles, and it's just expected that you will have charged through it over the course of the summer before the exam. I found it to be pretty overwhelming, because it was simply not possible for me to read everything on the bibliography. So there's all this anxiety; will I be quizzed on this one thing that I didn't read? I just did the best that I could in preparing for both the exams and the prospectus. Of course in retrospect you wish that you had been more prepared somehow, someway.

So I passed my generals, and then I had a meeting with my advisor, who offered me an evaluation, highlighting the strengths and weaknesses of my performance. It was a routine part of the process; once all the other examiners have left the room and they've decided whether or not to pass you, your advisor invites you back into the room for further evaluation. I had a nervous breakdown, actually, after that conversation. After my advisor gave her spiel, the first words out of my mouth were "I'm so exhausted," and I just started sobbing because I had been given further instruction as to how I would remedy whatever deficits I had. I was told that I needed to go back and make sure that I had read *every single thing* that was listed on the bibliography, and that I was to audit a couple of lecture courses on certain topics covered in the bibliography. The thought of being given a tremendous load of work, after having completed what I thought was already an overwhelming amount of work—I guess it was just like the straw that broke the camel's back. It was like, really? I thought that passing the exam was acknowledgement that I had done sufficient work and had given a satisfactory performance, but it certainly didn't feel that way. I felt like I passed on paper, but not in reality. It triggered this backlog of feelings from the first few years of my program that no matter how hard I worked, my efforts were never good enough, I would never know as much as my peers or my professors.

It took me a few days of crying and not leaving my apartment before I could think about what it meant for my future. But, after those few days, I said, all right, what else is there for me to do? What else do I have going on? Might as well. So I got back in the saddle and I said, okay, I've got one more semester of this and I'm going to do what they told me to do and I'm going to write a great dissertation on something that's of special interest to me. So I just kind of gave myself a pep talk after, of course, speaking with family and friends and taking in their encouragement and feedback, and I just moved forward knowing that this process would one day come to an end, that it wasn't forever.

After that I moved back to California for a year to start my research. It was a good decision as I felt less stressed—like I'd gotten out of the pressure cooker environment. Writing the dissertation was a liberating experience for me, because I was finally able to focus on a topic of special interest to me. I knew going into it that whatever drafts of chapters I produced would not be perfect—the goal at that point is just to get your ideas out knowing that they'll be reshaped over the coming years—and that took some pressure off as well. But, after a year I decided it was time to move back to my grad program. There were certain resources that would be easier to access—including my advisors, and a therapist, which my insurance didn't cover if I was away from the university. I missed New York and the museums there. Once I made the decision it was easy enough to go. I'd met some unanticipated challenges over the past year in California that made it clear to me that no matter where I went stuff happened, so if I was going to encounter difficulty I might as well do it in the environment that was optimal for completing my dissertation.

My last two years were peaceful and solitary. I was very good about completing work on my dissertation every day, keeping a timetable, and making good on my deadlines. I limited my contact with others, so there was no social conflict to contend with in conjunction with completing the dissertation. My advisors were great, responsive, interested in my project, and eager to help me finish. I think I was able to be so disciplined about the work because I really wanted to be done with my dissertation. I was ready to be done with graduate school, to get a job, to make more money. Graduate school creates this kind of extended adolescence that can go on and on, and I was ready to grow up.

At the end I was finishing and applying for jobs and post-docs at the same time, which was intense. I didn't cast a wide net, just one job and two post docs, but the fact that I'd applied for so few compounded the pressure. The Ivies represent a brand that carries with it a certain unspoken promise that if attended, you're set. You're going to get a great job, and your future is secure. But I guess people don't realize how competitive the academic job market is, which is something that I had to explain to my parents. When I applied for the job this past fall, my mother and father both said, "Oh, you'll get it." When I didn't, I think that they were really surprised.

Defending my dissertation was a very productive experience. My committee offered comments on my project with a spirit of encouragement and with the purpose of moving my project forward. It was much more positive, and far less anxiety provoking than my exams had been—partially, I think, because I was more confident, but also because my advisors were more confident in me. They knew I'd done the work and met the requirements; I'd already proven myself. Right on the heels of my defense, I found out that one of the postdocs had come through which was great timing, because I was certainly worried at that point about finding employment. You've got this degree in hand and you're like, is it worth anything if I can't get a job? What's the point of having a degree if you can't get a job? I have a PhD but I'm homeless!

For some people, finishing and graduating is a big cathartic moment, but it wasn't for me. I didn't feel much of anything. I just knew that I had more work to do over the summer: I had to find a publisher for my dissertation, plan the courses that I was going to teach in the fall, and I needed to try to get an article published. There was already work waiting for me after I had jumped over this hurdle of completing the PhD. So it just felt like one in a line of things that I needed to do. It took six years, beginning to end, but they flew by. I'm glad it's over! I think it would help people to hear more stories about what grad school life is like. People need to know, you're not crazy; it's not just you!

Moving On

I'm super excited to be working with new colleagues in my postdoc department; they produce work that was required reading for me throughout my graduate program and that I esteem pretty highly. I'm excited to move to a new city. I've heard great things about it, that it's a politically charged environment full of smart, interesting people. I'm really looking forward to jump starting my academic career.

I hope in a few more years I'll be in a tenure-track position at a research institution hopefully having published my first book. East Coast or West Coast, I made my peace with the

East Coast so I'd be okay with moving back. I would definitely hope to be married and have started a family by then—
maybe have one child. Beyond that? A new non-grad student
wardrobe; the option to live somewhere other than a student
apartment; more romantic dinners; more vacations to exotic
places...

Interview: Kathlyn "Kara" Cooney

Associate Professor, Egyptian Art and Architecture

Actor, Writer, Producer: *Out of Egypt, Digging for the Truth, Secrets of Egypt's Lost Queen* (among others)

Who is "Kara Cooney, Egyptologist" and how is she different from Kathlyn Cooney?

I use a different name depending on what I'm doing. Kathlyn is my formal name, and that's what I use in academic contexts. So, in my scholarly books and articles, I'm Kathlyn M. Cooney—or Professor Cooney if I'm in the classroom. Kara's always been my nickname, so I use it in less formal situations—with friends and family, or if I'm meeting someone in a cafe. So, just naturally, "Kara" became the name I would use when I was doing professional stuff that wasn't academic in nature—my television shows and documentaries, and my popular books, for example. I'm not sure if it's just in my own mind, to keep my identities straight, or if it helps clarify the way I'm presenting myself to the world…

What did you want to be when you were growing up?

I didn't really know what a professor was until much later in life, but I always knew I wanted to be a teacher. Still, when they asked this question in the second grade at Saint Michael's Catholic School all the girls said they wanted to be teachers—probably because those were the only role models available to them. So I said I wanted to be a nun. I remember thinking, oh no, everyone is going to be a teacher! I have to find something else, something a little different. So I guess my first inclination in life is to always try to do things a different way, and my second inclination is to be a teacher. It wasn't until I was wrapping up undergrad and applying for the Marshall scholarship that I realized that being an Egyptologist was a career track and that it involved teaching. It brought a number of things together for me: my love for being different, for teaching, and for all things old and dead. Thank god I did it in the mid-1990s because if I had tried to do that today I know that some professor would have been like, "You're crazy, there're no jobs; what are you thinking?"

Was it a straight shot from there to being a tenure-track professor?

Not at all. I got my PhD in 2002, and I came out to UCLA to teach for a year and was short-listed for an Egyptology job that was pretty well-suited to me. When I didn't get it, I was devastated. Instead, I did a three-year teaching post-doc at Stanford and tried to keep up with publishing, along with the teaching responsibilities. The years at Stanford were really hard for me—my husband was still in Los Angeles—and when I was asked to stay on for a fourth year I declined and came back to Los Angeles. I had no job, collected unemployment for eight months, and applied for anything related to a nonprofit that would be remotely suitable. I ended up working at the Getty for two years, and it was an interesting, complicated experience. I was a young scholar, with a good job and a decent salary, and an office with a view of the ocean. I got some research done, and found time around the edges of my job to finish my book. But most of my time went to facilitating the research of visiting scholars who were all doing what I wanted to be doing—working at research universities, and writing books on their sabbaticals. I applied to every Cal State that had a job up while I was on the market, and I got nothing. If I had gotten something, I would have thrown myself into the teaching and service they require, and would have loved it, but if I'd gotten one of those jobs, I don't think I would have been a contender for research university jobs later because I wouldn't have had time to keep up with my publishing.

How did you handle the idea that you might not reach your professional goals?

I was okay with it; not thrilled, but okay. I'm married to a screenwriter and producer; that's a really volatile line of work so having steady employment and benefits was ultimately more important than anything else. In this economy? Even if you're not doing exactly what you were trained to do, having a job with a salary and benefits is incredibly valuable—more so, for me, than scraping by and relentlessly holding out for what you have a passion for. Without a safety net you will not only burn out, but also you will end up getting sick and not being able to take care of yourself. You could end up really bitter, or worse, you could end up homeless and living in your parents' basement. I never believed in following my passion at all costs.

Fortunately, however, another position opened up at UCLA and this time, it worked out. This job means having my cake and eating it too. There's a lot of teaching and service, which are so important. But there's also time for research—there's support and funding, and I can get things done. So, as far as bumps in the road, I had a few. Waiting seven years after grad school to get my first research professorship—that's actually pretty common, as is, I suspect, eight months of unemployment. But I'm living my dream now, and because of the bumps in the road, I am—perhaps—more grateful for my situation than I might have been otherwise. I still occasionally have that desperate fear that someone is going to yank it all away because it's so amazing to be here at UCLA in the first place.

When did Hollywood start knocking on academia's door?

While I was at Stanford I co-curated LACMA's Tutankhamun exhibition. It was a high-profile show, and I ended up giving tours to a bunch of celebrities including Ethel Kennedy, who was there with some of her children and grandchildren. At the time I didn't think much about it; I was just having fun with the tour and doing my shtick. But their tour group included a guy who was in the industry. This is the way things work in Los Angeles! He saw me give the tour and thought I was pretty good; that I could talk to people and get them excited and interested in what I was doing. A year or so later—right at the time when I was unemployed—he got in touch and asked if I'd do a documentary in Egypt about the female king Hatshepsut. Of course I said yes, being unemployed. There was money involved, and that was a big deal! We were so poor at the time, we were clipping coupons, and we never went out to eat. I saved everything I could from that show, including all the per diems. On the last day of shooting when I was heading back to Cairo, the producers didn't have time to book a hotel so they gave me $400 in cash for meals and lodging. I flew with the sound guy, who lived in Cairo, and we'd been working together for a couple of weeks at that point so we had a good rapport. He was a really nice guy and he invited me to stay with him and his sister so I didn't have to spend the money. I said, hell yes, and stayed with the guy and his sister so that I could keep my $400 dollars. To this day there are rumors that I had an affair with the sound guy because I never checked into my hotel! That's the kind of thing I wouldn't do today, understanding how stories can spread, but then I just needed the money.

Did you think of the Hatshepsut documentary as veering away from the traditional path?

Through my involvement with the Tutankhamun exhibition I had started doing some work as a talking-head and found out, over time, that I was good at it. More importantly, though, I live in Los Angeles and that alone puts me in contact with all kinds of people who work in media. The blockbuster Egypt exhibition here meant giving tours to celebrities, and in my case, I ended up giving a tour to Craig Ferguson, host of *The Late, Late Show*, and ended up on his show two weeks later. That's the kind of thing that couldn't just happen anywhere. Also, I'm married to someone who specializes in media work; he knows the entertainment industry; and he knows how to present oneself in a way that delivers meaningful content that is also understandable, popularizing, and engaging. We've been together for a long time; he's know me from the very beginning when I couldn't give a public talk to save my life without my heart jumping out of my chest and my hands shaking for all to see. Public presentations used to scare me beyond belief, and he helped me to overcome my fears by letting me practice every conference paper. He was relentless; he knew how nervous I was and put me through my paces. So, basically, I've been in a kind of "media training" for a long time—long before I started doing actual media. And it's not like the practice and the training helped me fix my weaknesses; I still have them, but I know what they are, and I know how to compensate for them in ways that help shift attention to my strengths.

If you ask how one can broaden the academic path enough to engage in more nontraditional endeavors that aren't straight-up academic work, I think that a lot of the answer lies in having the confidence to do it. You want to impart information in a way that's free and joyful and inviting and inclusive. And those descriptors are all quite contrary to how academia usually urges us to share information. Presenting oneself to the public is a very emotional thing; a lot of academics are too nervous to make a public statement without notes, or without carefully conferring with the right colleagues—and that's not how television works. I'm not trying to say I have all the confidence in the world, or that I have all knowledge at my fingertips—because I'm actually quite a hesitant person in terms of my belief in my own knowledge abilities—but I have seen behind the curtain enough to understand that these very different audiences work according to different rules. I've also seen behind the curtain enough to know that most academics don't watch TV, so there's nothing to be afraid of! Or if they're predisposed to criticism, that's how they're going to respond regardless of whether you're giving a paper at a conference, or making a guest appearance on a talk show. If you get some satisfaction from it—from speaking to a broader audience—then what does it matter, how they respond. Life is too short; do it anyway.

When did you switch from taking advantage of right-place, right-time opportunities, to pursuing media work more proactively?

My first few opportunities were pure chance, but after the Hatshepsut documentary I found an agent who worked on finding other documentaries for me to work on. He put me up for my next big project, *Digging for the Truth*, and they flew me out to DC for an audition. It was the most absurd thing; I was working for a research institute during the week, and flying to DC to audition over the weekend. They put me in a forest, gave me a piece of flint, and asked me to start a fire. I'm like, "I don't know how to start a fire." I'm trying, and it's not working, but they're not giving up. "Go on, start a fire! We really want to see you have success in this." Like emotional support was going to take the place of a totally absent skill set! Finally they gave up, and asked me to tell them something about archaeology and the ancient world. I started talking, just being me, and they liked it. They put together a team of people: two host-y guys who were really cute and knew how to ask questions and present information, a weapons technical specialist, a guy who could do some scuba and survivalist stuff, and then there was me, the archeologist. I got to fly first class to Turkey—that was pretty awesome. And on another episode, I worked with a Civil War submarine in South Carolina, interviewing people doing underwater archeology. That episode won Emmys, so I hear; I mean, it was really fun. It didn't matter what the subject was—in fact, I was better on subjects that I knew nothing about because I could be fresh, I could be naive, I could ask the same kinds of basic questions that the viewers were probably asking and not feel embarrassed about it. I only had to be away for, like, six days at a time so I was able to make it work with my job by using vacation days. *Digging for the Truth* was really useful for me because I wasn't in the spotlight, I was just one of the subsidiary team members, so I learned a lot, without having a lot at stake.

After that show went off the air, I was asked to audition for a show called *Treasure Hunters* where you essentially would go around the world digging shit up, looking for treasure. I remember finding this out at the audition and saying, "I cannot do this. Do you understand? I can't do a show like this. It's unethical." And they were like, "No you'd be great, you're great for this. We'd love to have you." But as a reputable cultural archaeologist, I knew it was a mine field of ethically complicated situations. So there have been times when media opportunities have been available and I have turned them down because I knew, long term, that they would be stupid moves—bad for my academic career. And I've been able to be selective, because I've always had two things going simultaneously—a job and the media thing—except for those eight months of unemployment.

What kinds of opportunities were you looking for after *Digging for the Truth*?

The fact that I enjoyed that show so much contributed to my next big project—which was working with my husband to pitch a show to the Discovery Channel. We called it *The Travelling Egyptologist* at first, and the idea was that I would ask an anthropologically informed question in Egypt, then travel to eight or nine different places around the world to try to come up with some kind of answer. My husband and I wrote it together, and we worked really hard to come up with sample episodes and a strong prospectus. We pitched it to Discovery—and they bought it! We got to go around the world and we did six episodes; things like why are religion and violence so closely intertwined, why do people build pyramids all over the world, how was the devil created, and what did people think about evil before that? We did it the way we wanted to, for the most part, and I really learned a lot from seeing all these sites, from talking to all these experts all over the world.

But, I also learned that I don't fit what TV wants right now—though I probably could have made a really good go at this in the 1990s when documentary work was more traditional. By the time we aired in 2009, reality TV had already taken over and they wanted us to pump out content at a frequency that just wasn't possible. I'm not going to give up my day job, ever, and that means I don't have the time to produce that amount of content. As a woman, my chances of doing television into my late forties are incredibly slim, whereas in my day job at UCLA—as a scholar, professor—the experience that comes with age is valued. So, when Discovery told us our show was too educational, I accepted it—I had no interest in changing the show's premise to meet different demands. And now channels like Discovery and History and National Geographic are all producing almost pure reality content, and I'm not interested in that. So I'll wait. I'll bide my time until another television opportunity comes along that's appropriate for me. And I won't freak out if it doesn't.

With television on standby, have you found other ways to connect with a broader public?

Yes! So my next big nonacademic project is a popular book on Hatshepsut—an unusual figure in Egyptian history who ruled as a female pharaoh. It's an ideal project for right now because I can do it exactly the way I want to. The world of trade books requires an agent, and I was lucky because an agent who had seen some of my television work approached me about doing a book project and he really helped me find my way to this topic. I ran a couple of ideas past him first that were interesting, but more academically informed and I could tell that he didn't see "blockbuster" in them; he didn't see dollar signs or popular appeal. Finally, he was the one that suggested a biography of Hatshepsut. At first, I was resistant—that's not what I do, that's not my area at all; I thought he only mentioned it because of the documentary I'd done on the same subject years earlier. He told me to just think about it. And then he added that he thought the topic could attract a generous contract. And that caught my attention. Los Angeles is an expensive city, especially when you're thinking about buying a house, and paying for preschool. And supplementing my income with side jobs has worked well for me before. So we talked about it; we talked about gender roles, and power, and other things that were interesting to me, and before too long I saw the value in the idea. The stumbling block for me was that, as a Humanities professor, books are the most essentially academic thing you can do and I thought that any book I did had to be closely aligned with my scholarly profile. But once I realized that this was really, truly, a different type of book, I was able to disassociate this popular book from my academic track.

I like being an academic slash journalist, and the Hatshepsut book for me is, in a way, like exploring the Hunley submarine. Egyptology covers thousands of years, so I can honestly say that Hatshepsut is not at all my field, but that fact also liberates me to ask different kinds of questions that are going to be interesting to a more general readership. But I'm not a journalist, I'm an Egyptologist, so I'll get my bearings in this new material much faster. And because it's not my area, I don't have a horse in the race. I don't have anything to prove, or a chronology to prove, so I can really focus on telling a good story. I don't have to generate new scholarship, because that's not the point—the point is to use the scholarship we already have to create an accessible, engaging, narrative. I really love the process of creating narrative history for the public. I didn't know I would love it so much, and I never would have found out if my agent hadn't come to me and led me to the project.

Is the book likely to have an impact on your academic career, even though it's disassociated from your research area?

You know I didn't think that *Out Of Egypt*, our television show, was going to be useful for my job but it helped me more than anything. I didn't include it in my tenure dossier, but the committee wrote to me and told me to add it. I got all nervous, thinking oh no, that doesn't belong there, no, no, no. But in the letter I got, confirming tenure, they praised the television show and mentioned how wonderful it was that a professor would make the effort to communicate to the public in a relatable way. That was the first time I'd ever put these two tracks together for my benefit. With this book, my instinct is to keep them separate—the academic and the popular—but you never know, it could happen again.

You were really nervous when the committee asked you to put the show in your dossier; what did you think would happen?

If I were at a different university with a different culture, I'm not sure they'd appreciate me stepping outside of strict academic rigor to engage in more popular work. There might be a greater risk of misperception—that I'm doing this for my ego rather than, as is actually the case, because as much as I love my academic work I also enjoy having a creative/intellectual outlet beyond what academia permits. Traditional academia doesn't allow the space to ask big, crazy, stupid questions, or to puzzle through something without a precise and elegant argument. There isn't room, and there certainly isn't time, for musing—intellectual musing. So for me, going outside of academia to television, or to popular books, lets me ask questions in a way that is, comparatively, unrestrained, joyful, and free. I think it might be an even bigger challenge for women in academia, since mothers tend to have more responsibilities vying for their limited professional time or because some might misjudge a woman's intent to be involved in popular endeavors. There's more at stake in using precious time for pursuits that deviate, even slightly, from the traditional path.

What's next for Kara Cooney, Egyptologist?

Well, as I mentioned, it was a surprise to me to find out how much I loved the process of writing a narrative biography, a story, for a trade press; there was a lot of creative value in the experience for me, as well as academic and intellectual value and I hope others see that as well—we'll find out. I'd definitely like to do another project like this, and hopefully sooner rather than later. It actually corresponds very nicely with my current academic book project which is so big, that it could be quite a few years before the monograph is ready—though, of course, I'll be producing articles along the way. So if it takes a chunk of time for me to get my next academic book out, it could be really nice to have a few more of these trade books come out along the way. It's also nice, when you have a secondary source of income, that you don't have to wait for a raise if you're ready for a bump in income. It's good to feel like I'm in charge of my own financial destiny.

I would consider doing television again, but only if I was a producer. Because, again, I'm not doing it to be famous, and my livelihood doesn't depend on it, so I'm not willing to do it at any cost. If the right thing comes along, it's possible. Of course everything changes when you have a child. Do I want to drag him around the world with a film crew? Would that be good for him, or bad for him? I don't know, but it's something that I'm open to. Never say never.

Sidebar 1: What It Took to Get It Done

"Trying to write this fucking dissertation is like trying to squeeze water out of a rock."

"Getting it done was the culmination of thousands of baby-steps. I chiseled away at the dissertation for years, and one day, miraculously, it was finished."

"My graduate work always reminds me of my daily runs. Sometimes it was hard, sweaty, and taxing. In those moments, I would recall my feet hitting the pavement, one after another, to finish my run. That's what saved me, the knowledge that if I kept going, forcing one foot in front of the other, I would complete my PhD."

"I used the Pomodoro Method, a productivity tool shared with me by a fellow grad student; it was helpful because the project was never about 'writing a dissertation,' but instead about doing a small task for twenty five minutes. Toward the end when I was getting tired, I ended up breaking down the segments of work into seven to ten minute chunks. It wasn't graceful, but it got the work done."

"In the final months, after I broke down crying on the phone with my mother (my advisor had chastised me over a sketchy chapter), she rented me a car so I could spend a weekend far away, writing. She also hired a psychic to counsel me long-distance, while I ate bad Indian takeout in a crummy hotel room in the middle of nowhere. But it worked. After reconnecting with my inner child (more tears), I churned out my introduction. And then the rest was not so tough."

"I hired an editor to review everything before I sent it to my committee. She dotted all of the Is and crossed all of the Ts that I had missed. When I sent my dissertation to my committee, they commented on how refreshing it was to read such a polished draft, and they were able to sign off immediately."

"I had a great writing partner who was at the same stage and read my work."

"Ben and Jerry's Vanilla Caramel Swirl."

"A very regular and active fitness regimen that I genuinely enjoyed—yoga, walking, hiking."

"In the last six months my committee requested a ton of extra experiments. I ordered hundreds of mice and filled all the incubators with cells on an industrial scale never before seen by that lab. It was a quantity, not quality, approach—some sort of bulldozer method that required working sixteen hours a day and spending who knows how much lab money."

"I can still remember realizing over the Christmas holidays, if I want to file this spring, I have to start working six and seven days a week. I remember telling my husband—who was totally on board, even though it meant he was basically the sole parent to a three-year-old and a six-month-old—and that's what I did. I worked six days a week for two months, and then seven days a week for another two months. I defended my dissertation on my daughter's first birthday and walked the next day."

"Really what propelled me to finish was getting a tenure-track job and knowing that I needed to get it done before I started working—because I'd never have time for it after. There is nothing like that kind of pressure to get things going; better than eighteen espressos a day."

"Hypnotherapy (two rounds), threats of being sequestered in one of my committee member's basements until I had finished, and multiple writing groups."

"Every time I saw my grandmother she'd tell me that she was afraid she'd die before she saw the only member of her extensive family receive her PhD. That weighed on me pretty heavily!"

"I submitted abstracts to CFPs strategically so that over the course of about two years I gave five conference papers, each of which corresponded with a chapter of my dissertation. It was stressful to take time away from the dissertation to write a conference presentation, but really helpful in the long run as I ended up with a twelve-page head-start (and some feedback from the conference) for every single chapter."

"Different strategies worked for different chapters. My most productive period was when I'd go to the library at 9:00 p.m. and write until it closed at 2:00 a.m. Some people swear by writing first thing in the morning, but for me it was easier if I'd gotten all the little stuff out of the way. Also, there are very few distractions in a library at midnight!"

"In the end, the only thing that worked was eliminating every source of pleasure from my life—contact with friends and family, good food, exercise, nonacademic reading, TV. Facing such a bleak existence forced me to write my way out of my self-created misery. My partner was away for the last few months of writing and I'm glad—to this day—that he didn't see me in that state."

"I did most of my writing at a research center run by people with a real appreciation for good coffee in the morning, wine with lunch, and, to my happy surprise, port in the afternoon. Since I was not used to drinking in the afternoon, the lunch-time glass of wine followed by a healthy glass of sweet, rich port would get me through a solid afternoon of writing. Nothing like alcohol to loosen inhibitions (and make one write...)."

"Three iced venti mocha lattes with extra whip per day; always on an empty stomach."

"I took an unofficial year off and pursued some creative projects—writing fiction, working on an independent film—all while submitting inflated progress reports to my committee. I was terrified that I was turning into a cliché—how many grad student dropouts tell themselves they'll just take one year off? But I came back refreshed, and having some nonacademic accomplishments under my belt made me feel better about being an academic—like I was choosing it, rather than trying to survive it."

"The night before my (firm) deadline, I still had a lot of work left to do, when the power cord for my laptop bit the dust. In the five minutes before my battery died, I saved everything onto a thumb drive and raced to the computer lab. It was a long way from my place and we were in the midst of a blizzard. My hands were so raw from the cold that my knuckles actually started bleeding. I was so tired that, at one point, I almost headed home to take a nap. At the doorway to the lab I stopped; I knew that if I went to sleep I would miss my deadline. But my better angels saved me, and I didn't."

Part II

PhDs Beyond Academia

Chapter 4

Anika
PhD, American Studies
Writer, Creative Nonfiction

Finishing the proposal, getting an agent, and selling my book was an absolutely defining moment for me; it provided a kind of validation that meant more than I can express. I did it on my own, and while it's a departure from what academia would have me do, it's a return to what I've always felt in my heart.

Getting There

I didn't think about going to graduate school until practically the last day of my senior year in college. After I defended my thesis, all four of my professors said, "Why on earth didn't you apply? You would love it. You'd be a natural, you have a scholarly bent." I felt betrayed at that moment. Of course they meant it as a compliment, but the answer to their question was that no one had ever mentioned the possibility to me. I had no mentoring, whatsoever.

During high school, I knew I wanted to go to a small, private, liberal arts school, but it was up to me to figure it all out. No one was counseling me or coaching me on the matter—teachers, guidance counselors, parents least of all. I did it all on my own—researching schools, applying, getting in. I got a lot of financial aid, but my parents helped out when the financial aid didn't cover all of the expenses. It must have been really hard for them, but they never said anything. I don't even remember them asking me, "What are you going to major in?" Sometimes I express this as a feeling of neglect, and I resent that they never mentored me. But I shouldn't think of it that way. They never put pressure on me; they gave me perfect freedom—there was no question that it was my decision and not theirs. I can't imagine what it must be like for people who are pressured by their parents to choose a major or a career. Sometimes I wish they'd been more interested in my process and choices, but I think I benefited from their hands-off approach far more than I lost out. It made me really independent.

The fall after I graduated from college I moved to join my then-boyfriend, now-husband, who was doing a PhD in the sciences, and started working at a university press. I'd thought I was going to work in scholarly publishing and that it would satisfy my scholarly bent. I loved the idea of editing manuscripts and reading and commenting on other people's writing, of acquiring and curating a list of books, and exercising judgment about what's worthy of being published. I love, love, love the idea of nurturing people, of seeing books in manuscript form rather than in book form, and discovering talented authors. I thought I'd work my way up the ranks until I could be an editor. I thought I'd move over into trade publishing eventually and work for one of the big houses in New York. Editing offered a well-defined, well-structured career path and I liked that.

After a year at the university press, I moved to New York. I found a job in Manhattan, and an apartment in Brooklyn, and I was making a go of it in the big city. I thought I'd be going to cocktail parties filled with literary people and having scintillating conversations about novels that no one else had even read yet because they were so new. I was going to be plugged into the literary scene. The whole thing—the work, the lifestyle—was very attractive to me, but it was only attractive as an idea. In practice, I was pretty miserable. I didn't love the city, and I didn't love either of the publishing jobs I had while I was there. They weren't creative, and they weren't scholarly; they were just jobs. The romance faded pretty quickly.

After my professors suggested grad school, I started thinking more and more about it. I applied for the first time while I was still working at the university press. When I didn't get in, I thought, okay, I got that out of my system. It wasn't meant to be. But the idea didn't go away, and after trying two different jobs in New York, I realized that scholarly publishing was not satisfying the urge to produce scholarship on my own. I applied again, and the second time I got in. In all, it was a three-year process from when I left college to when I started grad school.

I chose an American Studies program rather than an English Literature program for a number of reasons, but one I remember vividly involved a conversation with a professor during a campus visit. She said that, for her, the big difference between a lit department and an American Studies department was that in American Studies you have primary, immediate contact with archives, with history. You don't get that in literature, which is about a text that has already been discovered, published, and framed for you. She talked about the kinds of discoveries you can make in the archives and described it as a process full of serendipity and surprises—not just analysis, which is the primary investigative tool for literature.

On a practical level, American Studies represented a break from the canon of English literature; the interdisciplinarity promised freedom—more time to learn what I wanted to learn, and less time spent learning what other people thought I ought to know. Also, by then, my husband and I were ready to leave New York City, and the town where I ultimately went to grad school had opportunities for both of us.

Getting Through

For me, graduate school was never about choosing a career; it was about the experience. I was excited to make friends and take classes again, and was really looking forward to being part of a department and cohort. It felt like the first day of college, and I was eager to prove myself. I wasn't thinking about my future career, I was just relieved that I could postpone the question. For six years I could say, "I'm a graduate student." I was there to write a book—a dissertation. That's all I wanted to do, and I was getting paid to do it. It was phenomenal.

But the euphoria faded, and I started feeling pressure almost immediately. I had a hard time keeping up with the reading, as everyone does. In seminars, I felt like I was involved in conversations that had started years before, without me, and I was completely unprepared for them. I realized pretty quickly that there was a big difference between the education I'd received, and the education a lot of my peers had received at Ivy League schools; they were introduced to canons, critics, and philosophies that I'd never encountered. I felt like a remedial student, perennially behind and undereducated, and having to hide it all the time. What I remember most from the first two years is staring at a page in a thick book, paralyzed by anxieties, constantly second-guessing myself, and trying to read as fast as possible at the same time. "I don't understand; I should read whatever came before this so I get whatever it is that this book is referring to in shorthand. No, I can't do that, I don't have time—I have to read this. But I don't understand…" My mind would lock up. I lived in a constant state of anxiety and had frequent thoughts of quitting, not because I didn't like grad school, but because I didn't feel like I was good enough.

I'm not a neurotic person; a lot of my anxieties were legitimate. I really was behind a lot of my peers. But when you meet with a professor, you can't confess to feeling like you're behind—much less to feeling debilitating anxiety. You can't show weakness. You still have to impress them even outside the classroom. It would've been nice if someone had offered some intellectual guidance: which books I could read over the summer to catch up, how to skim a book, how to take notes that would be useful later, how to prepare for a seminar. I remember being impressed by older graduate students but I never thought of them as resources because they were every bit as removed and untouchable as professors. It's a very real, practical problem because these are the people who will be writing letters of recommendation, and considering you for fellowships, jobs, or publishing opportunities. You want them to see you as nothing less than fully competent.

I made some good friends, and I talked to them about some of what I was going through, but I didn't feel like our anxieties were aligning. We complained about professors, about the lack of support in graduate school, and how hard things were, but I never felt like I was able to come clean about having a fundamentally inferior education, or about how I always felt behind and didn't know what they were talking about a lot of the time. Also, I listened to them express their anxieties, then watched them go back into the classroom and give brilliant performances, so I knew that they really did have the stuff to back up their claims of academic identity. Their anxieties were real, but they were, I don't know, coming from a different place.

I've talked to enough people to know that everybody feels like they have to hide how much of a fraud they are from the rest of the world. I knew it even before I started grad school. I had worked in scholarly publishing where I was the primary contact for academics who were publishing with our house, so I saw the flipside. I saw professors at their anxiety-ridden worst—when they needed their books for tenure. I knew that academia was a system designed to make people insecure about their intellects. But I still felt like the character of my anxieties was fundamentally different. "Sure, everyone's anxious but I *really* don't measure up. I really *am* worse off."

After coursework I had to take qualifying exams, which were hell on earth. I hate thinking about that time. I have a very, very bad memory, and when it comes to presenting, I am best in written form. But our exams were oral rather than written, so I knew I was going to do terribly, and the whole time I was reading, I was dealing with that pre-knowledge. I read two hundred books to prepare for the exam, and I knew I wouldn't be able to hold them all in my head all at once. I devised the lists myself—someone should have told me to pare it down so that I could do a better job with each book, but there was no advising. I never met with the four professors who gave the exam while I was preparing, not even once. The anxieties about the exam were always in my head—a voice I could not shut off. I did everything I could to prepare; I worked unbelievably hard. I'm proud of my work ethic, but when it came time for the actual two-hour exam, it was horrible. I knew it would be horrible. It was so mortifying to be that bad in front of four amazing professors.

And after that, I'm supposed to come up with a dissertation topic? The prospectus was a foreign genre to me. It wasn't clear how much I was supposed to know about my project in advance, and how much I would be allowed to figure out afterward and, again, there was no instruction or mentoring on the subject. I felt like I was flailing about, making things up as I went along. The prospectus defense was equally mortifying; I felt like they were rubber stamping me. It would've been less mortifying if someone had said "Your prospectus is not good enough yet, and it's not going to serve you well when it comes to writing the dissertation. Let's see what is good about it and make that better." I could've benefited from that kind of criticism. Instead, it felt like they were disappointed in me, but passing me anyway.

Things got a bit better for me in my fourth year; after the qualifying exam and the prospectus were over, the anxiety died down enough that I could put my nose to the grindstone and have a bunch of projects going at once. I spent the year teaching, being pregnant with my daughter, and writing a chapter. I also put together a conference panel with a friend, and published a couple of papers. I was trying to be professional about things. I struggled a bit with my chapter—trying to stake out some territory of my own in a very crowded intellectual field— but I generally enjoyed the analytic work of it all.

I planned to take a semester off to have my baby, but ended up taking a year off. After the first four months I went to talk to my advisor and told him that I didn't know what I was going to do, because I didn't have childcare lined up, and I wasn't ready—I mean, I was still nursing her. He was actually wonderful. It was a conversation that could have gone in a couple of different directions and he took it in a very supportive direction. He said, let's go see the registrar and find a way to make this happen. And she did. The grad school didn't have any policies in place to support maternity leave, but she found a way to stop the clock so I could take more time off without it counting against me.

I had another meeting with my advisor, later, to ask him for a letter of recommendation for a prestigious fellowship. He agreed to write the letter, but he also told me not to get my hopes up saying, essentially, that I couldn't compete with students who'd won the fellowship in the past, and citing two of my peers as examples. I remember thinking, "Well, fuck you. Yes I can." That was a crystallizing moment for me. My advisor wrote what must have been a great letter for the fellowship, and I won—which was phenomenally affirming. The award meant a lot financially, but more importantly, it was something that I could put on my CV. Maybe I felt inadequate in every seminar I took in graduate school, but I won this prestigious fellowship. No one can say that I'm not of the same caliber as Mr. X and Mr. Y, because I'm like them—they have the same line on their CVs.

I returned to grad school right after my daughter turned one. I was a grad student in the morning, mom in the afternoon, sometimes a grad student again in the evening. I was proud of the fact that I was doing full-time work on a part-time schedule, and I was keeping up with all the other full-time grad students who didn't have kids. But putting her in daycare was just horrible. It was so hard to leave her, and it was hard for me to believe that what I was doing when I wasn't with her was as worthwhile as being with her. I know many parents have that same experience. It's just fundamentally, exquisitely excruciating to take your special child who you know better than anyone in the world and hand her over to a stranger for whom your child is one of many and not particularly special. The teachers there, they've seen it all. The director told me she'd only cry for two weeks, but we were both miserable for at least five weeks and I didn't get anything done the entire time. I missed her and felt very guilty and all of the things that people feel. We eventually calmed down into what became a very good routine—working for a few hours each day and playing in the afternoons—but I remember how hard it was to get to that point and all those feelings are still there.

At the end of my fifth year, we moved to upstate New York. My daughter was just turning two and she started daycare full time in our new town. In my sixth year I wrote two chapters and finished my PhD. Before I moved away, I had a conversation with my advisor where I officially came out and said, "I am not going to apply for academic jobs." His response was "Oh, well it's not as if you applied to graduate school in bad faith or anything." Bad faith? I never promised I'd get a tenure-track job in academia!

I definitely felt him pull away at that point; I think he made a conscious decision not to invest his time in my dissertation because what would be the point? Moving didn't change much in terms of my access to mentors or resources. I was on my own, just working out of a different library. In the end, as much as I hated the rubber stamp during my qualifying exams, that's all I wanted from him. I just wanted him to sign off, and move me along. We just kind of ignored each other and that worked out. I submitted my dissertation remotely, and I didn't go to the graduation ceremony. It was all very anticlimactic.

Moving On

Toward the end of my fifth year in grad school, I'd had an idea for a book project. At first, I thought it could be a new direction for my dissertation but after I'd tried to sketch an outline, I realized it wouldn't work—not in that form. But the idea stayed with me. By the time I finished my dissertation, I knew I wanted to pursue a career as a writer. I'd published a chapter from my dissertation in a scholarly journal, but I'd also started writing non-scholarly pieces for a general audience and sending them out. I wasn't getting anything published, but I was definitely thinking about it professionally.

I found out that I was pregnant with my son just days before submitting my dissertation and just days before turning 33 years old, so I knew right away what my next big project would be-having my baby. My dream was that, in my thirty-third year, I would get a baby, a dissertation, and a book contract. I got the first two, but the book contract had to wait. When my son was born, I hadn't yet finished the proposal so I had to set it down for a while. I started a writing group with a friend, and read books on how to get a literary agent. After my son was born, I picked the proposal back up and we worked together; he'd sleep or nurse in a sling against my chest, and I would type; when he'd wake up I'd set aside what I was doing. My daughter went to daycare full time until I finished my dissertation, then part time afterward. That was a source of guilt and insecurity for me, since I wasn't doing anything that anybody else would recognize as legitimate—but, I loved having the time. I loved writing, daydreaming, and brainstorming; strategizing for the future felt very productive, even if I wasn't bringing in any money.

Telling the story in retrospect makes it seem linear—even simple—but it wasn't at all. I thought about what I would do if I didn't get the book contract. I considered adjunct teaching at one of the local universities or community colleges. Looking back, that just seems crazy—it would have made me miserable—but at the time it seemed like something I should consider. I thought about getting back in touch with the university press where I'd worked before grad school. I also looked into getting a job at a bookstore downtown. If I couldn't be a writer, at least working at a bookstore I'd be surrounded by books and people who loved books. But I was really casting about.

I knew what I wanted career-wise, but I was very conscious of how I was perceived by others. I thought I would look selfish for putting my child in daycare, while doing ostensibly nothing. Also, I didn't have a professional identity. Any time I had to fill out a form that asked what I did, I'd have to write "homemaker" and part of me died, because it's not what I was. Even if I had been taking care of my daughter full time, that's not how I would have wanted to identify myself. That was a year of deep uncertainty for me; it was a really hard time. The fact that I had a PhD meant absolutely nothing; I couldn't bring it up in conversation without provoking all sorts of questions—vocalized or otherwise—about why I wasn't doing anything with it. I had attained an incredibly difficult and hard-won level of achievement, but it was invisible and meaningless. I was proud of what I'd accomplished; I didn't want to inflate its importance, but it was hard to have gone through all that and not have anything professional to show for it—to not be a professor or some other kind of recognized post-PhD professional.

About six months after my son was born I finally finished the proposal. I started sending it out that summer, and in July I lined up an agent. My son started daycare a few months later. It was easier than it had been with my daughter because I had an agent, and it was only a matter of time before I was going to have a book contract. By that point, it definitely felt like I was on a career trajectory that was absolutely worth following. I didn't love him any less, but I was a somewhat wiser mom. It was still really hard, but I knew by then just how wonderful a daycare could be for a kid. I knew the difficult time would pass, and it wasn't as soul wrenching.

In September, I got the book contract. Finishing the proposal, getting an agent, and selling my book was a defining moment for me; it provided a kind of validation that meant more than I can express. I did it on my own, and while it's a departure from what academia would have me do, it's a return to what I've always felt in my heart. I have an identity now as both an intellectual, and a writer; the soon-to-be-published author of a trade book.

My contract gives me two years to write the book, and I assume it will take another year or so for it to be edited and to go to press. After that, the crystal ball goes dark. But I do know that I want to keep doing this. I want this to be my career, to write creative nonfiction, to tell true stories, creatively, in book form. I hope that in the course of writing this book, I will come across another idea for a book. And I hope that in the course of publishing this book, other opportunities will come my way. I want to be a writer, and I want to have so much momentum behind whatever niche I've carved out for myself, that I always have projects queued up one after another.

I was surprised by how much my degree meant when I was shopping my project around. I'd always thought that if you earned a PhD and then decided not to become an academic— well, then there were just no other careers available. If you had the nerve to try and pursue another career, your PhD would actually be a hindrance because you'd be simultaneously over-qualified and under-qualified. You'd look ridiculous, like a hippopotamus in a fish tank. In fact, I found that people in trade publishing were very glad to see I had a PhD because that was shorthand for my ability to start and finish a project, my research abilities, and my knowledge of archives. They didn't need to find out if I could do it because I'd already done it. All they needed to ascertain was whether or not I was a good writer, and those capacities were revealed by the book proposal.

I was told in several different contexts that being an academic who can write well is a powerful combination. Looking back, I don't know if I would change anything. I'm so glad I got a PhD. If I hadn't, it would've always been a regret. I'm extremely grateful that I found American Studies which is why I'm able to write history now. If I could impart some kind of wisdom to current graduate students, I'd suggest that they advocate for institutionalized mentoring. Match a fifth-year student up with a first- or second-year student. Talk about what kinds of tools you need to get where you want to go. I'd tell them that nobody knows what they're talking about; if they feel out of the loop, or behind, or insecure—so does everybody else. I'd tell them that they can do a lot of amazing nonacademic things with a PhD. If you have a story to tell, think about telling it in the form of a trade book because publishers are looking for that. I had no idea that there was a place in the market for that kind of writing, but there are a thousand people who are writing a novel in their spare time for every half-person who's writing narrative nonfiction.

Chapter 5

Gabriel
PhD, Art History
Museum Curator

At the end of the day, we all speak the same language. It's been interesting being a curator; I bring academics to my current institution to speak, and I don't see any gulf between us except that one of us is working for a popular audience, while the other is working for a student and academic audience.

Getting There

After finishing my undergraduate German Studies major, I spent a year in Dresden on fellowship teaching English and American Studies. I applied for master's programs while I was there, and the best offer came from a school that was close to home, and close to family—so I moved back to the Northwest. They didn't have a northern European specialist so I shifted my focus to American art. I didn't realize that it was a three-year master's program—they don't tell you that part—and they required two foreign languages before you could even start your thesis credits which makes it a minimum of three years. So I came in fluent in German, having just spent an entire year in Dresden, and I aced the language exam—but then I had to take two full years of French before I could even start my thesis credits. That served me well by the time I started my PhD program, but the time line was kind of daunting from the outset. I'd just spent three years getting a master's degree, and was looking forward to a minimum of six years more for the PhD. The idea that, oh my god, it would be nearly a decade before I would start my professional life—it seemed overwhelming.

At the end of my MA I was looking at doctoral programs, and one just made the most sense in terms of the quality of the program, the funding that was available, the resources on campus, and the collections. Again, they were without a faculty member in my area, but they were planning to find someone. So I ended up working with another professor for my first two years which actually turned out to be really helpful. It added an area of expertise that I wouldn't have had otherwise, and turned me into—to borrow from Broadway—a triple threat. It's a rare person who's been trained in multiple subspecialties and it's served me very well in my career.

Getting Through

My first couple of years were really intense, but not for the reasons I'd expected. My family's business—a wholesale beer and wine company we'd had since the 1960s—was failing. I was the sales and inventory manager, so I would get up in the morning and work on shipping truckloads of beer out of Milwaukee. I'd go grab a coffee, and then I'd go to seminar. It was a strange, bifurcated life: beer distributor by morning, grad student by the afternoon. It wasn't something I would have done by choice, but it was really necessary. By the second year the company was folding, which created a huge financial burden for my family. Suddenly, they didn't have a salary, they didn't have health insurance. For a while there, I was basically the only one with a steady source of income, namely my graduate student stipend. We used my credit cards when they needed medication. I had never imagined in my wildest dreams that I would be a provider for my family, let alone while I was in grad school, and not really able to provide for myself. I mean, graduate stipends are wonderful, and it was great for my own support, but they aren't meant to be stretched—not like that. So that was a tough start to things. Ultimately, it all worked out. They got back on their feet again, and are all happy now. But it was a pretty stressful time, on top of doing coursework which is stressful in its own way.

My third year in grad school was a really pivotal one for me. I was 29 years old, and decided to come out. A good friend of mine from high school and my master's degree years had come to visit to help celebrate my birthday; we went out to dinner with my housemate, who was a good friend from both undergrad and my PhD years—and an openly gay man. Between them, they knew basically my whole life story, and something about being with them . . . there was just this moment of clarity where I realized something had to change. Some people who are in the closet just lead a double life. They are not open about their sexuality but they date people or have boyfriends. I was in the closet and completely celibate. I was closed off to the possibility of a relationship. I don't really know why it was so hard on me, because my parents were totally fine with it, other than worrying about my safety. I think a lot of it had to do with perfectionism; I had always been a straight-A student, a goody-two-shoes. I always did everything right, on the straight and narrow. I didn't think being gay was part of that equation.

But what I started to realize was that not reckoning with it was going to destroy everything because it would be the death of me. I had loads of friends, but I always felt alone. I was starting to become very unhealthy and very miserable, and I just said, "Something's got to give." So I came out to my friends that night, and the next day, the day after my birthday, I called my mom and I came out to her.

In addition to reckoning with my newly avowed sexuality, I was reckoning with losing weight. My pediatrician when I was a kid had pretty much laid it out for me. He last saw me when I was 21 years old, and he said, if you don't deal with this weight, I don't give you much past 30; I think you'll be dead by then. I pooh-poohed it at the time—sometimes you don't feel your own mortality until it's too late. But on my twenty-ninth birthday I realized that I was killing myself; I weighed 435 pounds. I was building my own closet out of fat and flesh so that I would never have to deal with my sexuality; my sexuality and my morbid obesity were very much intertwined. Once I had that realization, and once I'd come out, I lost 100 pounds on my own. Then I had gastric bypass surgery and lost another 135. You'd think that would've solved everything and I'd be back on the straight and narrow toward finishing my degree. But there were a lot of things that came along with the weight loss that I didn't expect. Afterward, I had so much extra skin that I had excruciating neck and back pain. I remember my professors were always telling me to sit up at the seminar table, to stop slouching—but I couldn't, the weight was too much. I finally had a skin removal surgery, which had some complications. Then, there was the loss of identity. I'd been a fat man all of my life; I knew how to function in the world at that size. When I lost all the weight, I felt like I'd become anonymous with nothing that distinguished me. I was used to getting a certain amount of attention because of my weight, and I felt its absence. Just imagine having all of that play out when you are already living and working in incredibly close quarters with your colleagues and professors; there's not a lot of privacy or anonymity.

I think everyone kind of knows your business in grad school; your classmates are just constantly sizing you up. My program was pretty egalitarian in terms of funding, but even so, there's still the intellectual sparring that goes on in seminar or in classes, or even in more casual settings, if you're having dinner with a group of grad students and professors. Everyone wants to make an impression. I was lucky to have a very supportive community, and made many good friends. But it's just a difficult setting in which to have to go through anything of any major significance, because grad school, all by itself, can be pretty tumultuous; there's not a lot of room left for the personal ups and downs.

I postponed my qualifying exams because I'd had so much going on the first few years, which of course gave me more time to dread them. I remember being surrounded by books constantly, living with them, traveling with them. There was a point where I'd close my eyes and all I would see is pages of books. You're given a reading list a mile long, but you know you're not going to be asked about every book on the list because there's not enough time. So it's like a crapshoot. It's like studying for the devil's game of Jeopardy. Instead of Alex Trebek, it's Lucifer asking the questions, and you could be asked anything; you just don't know what the parameters are going to be. What I didn't realize at the time is that the faculty members, in most cases, are really invested in seeing you succeed. There are only a few times where I've heard of people being tricked by the faculty; when the exams have been used to administer a lesson. In most cases, they want to see you do well and to move on to the next stage, which is writing the dissertation. When I did finally take them and pass, it was like a weight was lifted. I felt almost the same sense of relief as when I came out of the closet.

So I'd finished my orals exams, but I hadn't produced any written work; I'd done all the research and had great research files, but I wasn't writing. At one point my advisor was trying to get a sense of how serious I was about finishing the dissertation or even starting it, because he hadn't received a chapter. We had a heart-to-heart; he saw that I was heading down a different path, toward museum work or commercial galleries or a major auction house. He told me that he thought I could leave the program at that point, without finishing, and still be successful. And he recounted examples of his own classmates who hadn't finished the PhD and were wildly successful in the art world in their chosen vocations. But the PhD wasn't just a means to an end for me; I needed to see it through to the end—to demonstrate my commitment to learning and research, and my ability to undertake a major writing project. I think he understood, but he was also taking a really practical approach to it by asking the big questions: Is this something you really intend to do, or want to do, or need to do?

I may have been clear about wanting to complete the PhD, but I wasn't always good at demonstrating it. I kept procrastinating. Much of it was through no fault of my own—family issues, health issues. But if I'm being perfectly honest with myself, there were nights when I could have stayed home writing when I went out, or went to New York for the weekend. That was partly because the writing years coincided with when I had my first ever boyfriend—which was a big deal. But there was also a point where I tried to run away from the dissertation. At one point I had run out of funding, and I applied for a fellowship that would have taken me to Europe to work on a major cataloging project. It was the kind of thing that would have provided valuable professional experience, but left little time for writing. I went to the interview, and one of the committee members—who recused herself because we knew each other—took me aside and said, you don't want this; you're just running away from your dissertation. I didn't get the fellowship, and I thanked her for it after I finished the dissertation. She did me the biggest favor. Otherwise, I think I would have run away—maybe forever—rather than confronting it head-on.

After more time had gone by and my advisor still hadn't seen any chapters, we had a big "come to Jesus" talk. He told me that my time was up, and he wouldn't allow me to continue in the program unless he had a chapter in his hands within 17 days. I did not take the news well. I broke down crying in his office. But I was grateful for the ultimatum, because—for lack of a better term—I manned up. I went home and I started writing, and I kept writing. I think my first chapter was the best chapter I wrote, and it was written under the most duress. I think that's typical of me; I do my best work when I've maxed out the procrastination, I'm the most stressed out, and am really under the gun. If I had it all to do over again, god, I would have started writing much sooner. In hindsight, there are things that I would have liked to have said or done with my dissertation that just simply weren't possible within that time frame—there wasn't a lot of time for revisions or finessing. I received some good advice while I was in the midst of all this. One of my professors told me that the dissertation was nothing but a series of seminar papers—of which I had written dozens by that point. He told me to treat each chapter like a seminar paper—to just get it done. "It's a glorified writing project" were, I think, his exact words. That was really helpful, because I'd been looking at the dissertation as this daunting, insurmountable task, when in fact it was completely surmountable by breaking it down into segments that were really recognizable to me in their scope. It doesn't need to be perfect. If dissertations were perfect then everyone would send them straight to the publishers right after the faculty approved them. That's never the case, and that's why it takes years to revise them. So it's okay to write an imperfect dissertation; in fact, everyone does.

One thing that helped so much during that time was having a writing partner—someone I really bonded with during those intense years, and with whom I remain close friends. He was preparing for the qualifying exams when I was dissertating—and since misery loves company, we'd camp out at Starbucks or one of the local coffee shops and work for hours. Sometimes we'd talk to one another, ask each other questions—but just having another person there who had the same kind of anxiety, the same deadlines and pressures was really, really helpful to me. I would go to work at my job all day, finish at five, come home and grab a quick dinner, then be over at the coffee joint by maybe six-thirty, seven o'clock. We'd work straight through until it closed, and then sometimes we'd grab a late-night snack, and then I'd go back to my dorm room and I'd keep working until I would either fall asleep or it would be time to get showered and go back to work. I pulled a lot of all-nighters; that was fairly routine. Sometimes I'd take my work with me to New York; I had a good friend who gave me a set of keys to his condo and I'd use it as a writing retreat when he was out of town on business. I'd bring mountains of work with me and camp out at The Big Cup, which has since closed, but was a sort of a legendary gay coffeehouse in Chelsea. I'd get a lot of work done there, then go out with friends for dinner, or go out on the town, and then do it all again the next day.

I look back and think to myself, oh my god, over the course of eight months, I wrote five chapters. In less than a year, I finished my dissertation. It took me seven years to complete the whole program, from start to graduation. Looking back, I wonder if I could have done it in six years, which was the prescribed amount of time. Maybe, if nothing else had happened in my life, I guess it's possible. But that said, only three of my cohort finished in seven years, everyone else took longer. I think six years is probably pretty ambitious—especially if your funding runs out and you get into the workplace, then you're slowed down even more.

In my final year, I was on fire. I had a job and was working the full number of hours we were allowed at that point. I was writing. I was dating. I had friends. I had a life. I felt like I was playing my A game. And I had the energy to do it. I had the drive and determination. A lot of that was because of the transformation in my health, in my physical being, that was occasioned by coming out of the closet and dealing with my weight. At the end, I was a much better and more thoughtful student for having reckoned with all that stuff, even though along the way it didn't seem like that would be the outcome. Along those same lines, I am really glad that I dealt with those things when I was in an environment where I had the benefit of full health insurance. Thank god. I mean, I think my grad school saved my life. If I'd been at another school that didn't offer health care to its grad students we wouldn't be having this conversation. I'm sure I would be a dead man.

It's interesting; the relief I felt at other stages, like passing the qualifying exams—I didn't feel that when I submitted my dissertation. I think I was too exhausted at that point. By then I was on the job market and tremendously fearful about whether or not I would find gainful employment in time. The minute you finish, the clock starts ticking. I was lucky in that my last job didn't end with the semester but continued through the summer which gave me a little more breathing room than most people, but it was still a tremendously stressful and anxious period in my life. You know a major episode is coming to an end, but you don't yet know what the next one's going to be.

Moving On

When I first got to grad school I actually thought that I was going to go into teaching, post PhD. But when I started working in one of the campus galleries, I caught the curatorial bug. I don't know why it didn't occur to me sooner; I've always collected, I've always been fascinated by the material world, by objects, by understanding what things are. I always went to museums growing up. When other kids were doing the things that kids like to do, I could be found in antique stores or history museums or art museums. I just love the world of objects and situating them in their historical contexts. It's such a natural fit; I feel so at home in the museum world. Being a curator is where my passions lie, and by the time I finished grad school I was 100 percent certain that that's what I was meant to be. It feeds all of my interests in research and writing, teaching, and working with objects and getting to know the material world, and making sense of it, and presenting it in context. I mean, everything I enjoy about art and learning about art I'm able to do as a curator. But I think grad schools—I think it's starting to change now, but there was a point where the history of art programs didn't really know how to deal with people who didn't want to be professors, and maybe didn't take them as seriously. Not across the board, of course. There were several professors at my school who really understood how important it was to train curators in addition to art history professors, but I wouldn't say that was a universal sentiment in the department. I felt some pressure around those issues at the time. People would make disparaging remarks about curators, suggesting that their curatorial colleagues were not held in the same esteem or the same regard as their academic counterparts.

Being on the job market had lots of ups and downs. I sent out scores of applications and didn't hear very much back. But then when it rains, it pours, and I suddenly found myself with a slew of interviews. It was like the good, the bad, and the ugly. I interviewed for one position where it turned out that I was the sacrificial lamb. They had an in-house candidate that they had already settled on hiring, but they needed to post the job and show that they were looking more broadly. I found that out very late in the game, but it was still a good experience to interview and to see a different institution, and to get to know the people there. I was a finalist for another good position that I ultimately didn't get. At one point, I was even interviewing for deanships. I learned that there isn't a lot of rhyme or reason to the job market. You can have a great set of credentials, a great résumé, and still not get an interview. Then sometimes you think you won't get an interview because you know the other people who are applying are more qualified, yet you get an interview, and you may actually get the job.

I'm glad I didn't lose faith, because just at the moment when I was starting to get the most discouraged, I found myself with three opportunities, not one. I ended up coming to a museum in the Southeast because I got to be a department of one, in a survey museum with colleagues in other fields—six curators in all. It's the best decision I ever made, and I'm very grateful for the opportunity because it fast-tracked my career. Had I gone to a larger institution I would have started as an assistant curator. I would probably still be an assistant curator there now, maybe an associate curator. But at my current institution, after two years, my position was made permanent, and I went from being a postdoctoral curatorial fellow to being a full curator. It accelerated my career in an extraordinary way, and other institutions—and headhunters—have started taking notice. My job is invigorating, but it keeps me incredibly busy. I have averaged, like, a flight and a half every single week for the last year in terms of my travels. Just from February of last year until the end of January this year, I flew 72 flights on commercial airlines, and another 12 on private. I've been traveling so much, I kind of don't know where I am. I'm not even exaggerating. I've been quite happy here, but I do eventually want to be an art museum director, and I know that in order to keep moving closer and closer to that goal, I need to take on positions of additional responsibility.

I think back to the occasional anti-curatorial bias I encountered in grad school, and it seems really distant now. At the end of the day, we are all art historians. We all speak the same language. It's been interesting being a curator. I mean, I bring academic friends and colleagues to my current institution to speak, and I don't see any gulf between us except that one of us is working for a popular audience, while the other is working for a student and academic audience. Yes, some people have pointed out that the creature comforts of being a curator are perhaps greater than those of being an assistant or associate professor. I don't know if you get to ride on a private jet once you become a full professor! Maybe there's a secret fleet…

This has also been a good place to live as a gay man in terms of finding an embracing community. There's a large gay community here, and even though some of my friends and family were worried about me moving here, I've not encountered prejudice. I will say that I've found it challenging to make friends, and I think it's because a lot of people here grew up together. They came out together. They have been each other's support for a very long time. It's not easy to be the outsider or the new kid on the block. I think I got used to living in a college town with a transient community where, if you're not willing to be friends with people who are only going to be there temporarily, you won't have any friends at all. Everyone you're around is coming from outside the community, or has been in that position at one time or another themselves.

They talk about the seven-year itch, and I am starting to think about the next chapter, and about the next city. I know that no place is perfect, but it would be kind of fun to be in a new environment and have the experience of discovering someplace anew. So I know that eventually, both for my professional and personal aspirations, I will end up leaving where I am now. But it won't be a happy departure; it'll be quite bittersweet.

Chapter 6

Kerry
PhD, Neuroscience
Patent Attorney

The best night's sleep I've ever had was the night after I said no to extending the postdoc. The idea that I never had to go back to that lab—that I never had to go back to any lab, anywhere—that I was free to choose anything else I wanted to do in life was just like, "Ahhhh . . . that's the first deep breath I've taken since I was eighteen."

Getting There

I always knew I would go to graduate school. My dad tells a story from when I was five years old; I was upset about something my parents had done, so I delivered the best ultimatum I could think of: "If you don't let me get my way, I won't get my PhD!"

I grew up in a small semirural college town in the Midwest where the main industry was the university. My dad was a PhD and all of my best friends' fathers were professors; I thought everyone went to grad school. My dad went to an office every day, but he came home early. He coached our soccer teams, and he had a lot of time for family. I didn't realize it then but after we went to bed he would continue working until midnight or 2:00 a.m. I was interested in science and after high school the next logical step was to go to grad school or to medical school. When I had to make a choice, I looked at my dad's life: he got to travel a lot, and he had good job security. A PhD seemed more logical than ever.

Of course, going to grad school wasn't just my idea; my parents encouraged me to follow in my dad's footsteps in a lot of different ways—some obvious, some more subtle. When my dad traveled for work, he always brought home Ivy League tee shirts as souvenirs. They became a kind of wearable list, representing the schools we would choose from one day. Even vacations were devoted to the Ivy League project. One summer we took a family trip to look at schools on the West Coast; then the next summer we made the same trip to the East Coast.

At the time, I couldn't separate my ambition from my parents'. I was eighteen. I wanted to do well. But in college you have to sink or swim on your own; you're the one who has to do the work. By the end of college, doing well had started to become my own ambition, but I still wondered whether I had given my choices enough consideration. From an early age, I was given subliminal messages: "You will do biology; you will do biology—here's another tee shirt for *your* collection." I was going down that path and because it all fit together so conveniently, it was kind of like, "Did *I* choose this?"

Biology, or more generally science, wasn't my first love—it was the practical choice. Music would have been the fun choice. I even visited conservatories at the same time that we were making the rounds of all of the colleges and universities.

I actually learned how to read music before I learned how to read English, and I think it had a fundamental impact on my brain. When I started music I was six years old. My teacher wanted me to learn to compose, so I started writing really bad music—sometimes several sheets at a time—which was more writing than I ever did in school. At the same time, I was teaching myself to read English by memorizing what the words looked like—because that's how you read music. My parents finally figured out that something wasn't right because I'd confuse words that looked very similar but sounded very dissimilar. They finally sent me to a language therapist who figured out that I was reading English like musical notation, rather than by using phonics. They got it straightened out, but I wasn't actually reading properly until fourth grade. But I was reading music when I was six, playing up a storm.

My parents always encouraged me, even though they thought of music as a hobby. But when my dad realized it could be a "hook" during the admissions process, he started to take it very seriously. During my older brother's Ivy League tour, he'd learned from other parents that kids needed the grades, but they also needed something else—some kind of unusual talent. Admissions officers would say, "we still have to field the football team, fill out an orchestra, produce a newspaper. Beyond the academic credentials, applicants need some other skill that will keep this university running and interesting." He thought my hook could be music—and then he got behind it, but only as part of an admission strategy.

That moment when I was 18 years old, deciding whether I should go to a conservatory or a university was really crucial. If you don't go to conservatory at that point, you can't do it later. You can't recapture that period of intense playing and development; those few years really do matter. I thought I would get to choose between science and music, but actually going to the conservatories put the kibosh on a career in music. During one trip, I was talking with two cello teachers and my dad was sitting there in the room. They asked me where else I was looking—and I now realize that they probably meant what other conservatories—but I gave them the list of universities. They just stopped in their tracks and said: "Wait a minute, you're looking at colleges? Good colleges? You can get into a really good college?" And I said, "I hope so, you know, I think so."

At that point they explained that anyone who could get into a good college should take that option, because they had ten amazing cello students, and one of them was going to get a job at a minor symphony or do other gigging work or take on millions of small jobs to piece together a livable wage. The other nine would wait tables the rest of their lives.

Getting Through

When I started my PhD program, I had simple expectations because I had two really simple goals: I was dead set on being a rock star during grad school, and becoming a professor. During the interview, they'd let a few of us in on a secret. Out of the 30 potential students who were interviewing, ten of us had already been officially accepted—forwarded to the dean's office, signed, sealed, done. The rest were contingent on the interview. It was nice to feel like one of the students they recruited—to be desired. I thought: This is great—they have the structure I want; I can pick a neuroscience lab and do the research I want; I'm on exactly the path I want to be on.

I had a pretty accurate idea of what my life was going to be like—or could have been like—for the next five years.

Undergrads had been treated like grad students where I went to college. I'd worked at a lab for two-and–a-half years; I had a desk in the lab and kept all my books there, I spent every minute I wasn't in class there. I worked for tough, kick-ass lab directors with high expectations. I ran the same kinds of research projects that a grad student would. I walked out with a Bachelor's thesis that was equivalent to a Master's thesis, and I felt like I had already been doing grad school for many years. I thought, if anything, that it would be easier now because after a year of coursework, I could do lab work full time. I'd get my papers out and then, bingo, a degree. I was ready.

I did have to sacrifice music immediately, and that was hard. One of the reasons I chose my grad school was because it was famous for cello, but it turned out that the seats were all reserved for undergrads or music school students—so after having an insane amount of music in my life for all those years, I came to grad school and it was completely silent. The absence of music made everything surreal. It was always the identity I had, not the one I was trying to earn, or had to try to explain. Without it, I felt like a huge part of my personality was gone. When something you've relied on for self-definition disappears, it changes everything—how you meet people, and how you feel about yourself. It makes difficult situations worse.

But my lack of identity and purpose were also related to grad school, because things weren't going very well with neuroscience. Over the summer our lab had exploded to ten people. We had orientation students who'd started to do little projects in our lab. It was a fun place to be; it was really active, my advisor was doing well. Then suddenly everything changed. I think it was triggered by the news that my advisor wasn't going to get tenure. He became a different person; he was incredibly unhappy. Things got so bad, eventually, that I had to talk to the director of my grad program and say "Either we figure out a way for this to work or I'm going to have to quit grad school. I can't take this anymore." The director said that he didn't want me to leave—that we needed some kind of probation period. But by that point, my advisor had decided that he wanted me out—immediately. It felt like a classic case of being stuck between a rock and a hard place. Am I quitting? Am I getting kicked out?

It was only the beginning of my third year. If I'd quit, and if I'd wanted to continue grad school somewhere else, the transition would've been difficult—and even if I'd made it, it would have set me back several years. Grad schools are not completely unforgiving, but they do want students who are going to stay and finish, not students who are going to quit after taking a couple of years of tuition-waivers and stipends. I would have had a lot of explaining to do, and it would have been hard to discuss the difficult relationship I had with my advisor. Plus, I would have had to start over again at the application stage. That's a lot of time to lose. I had already qualified, and the qualifying exam is so time consuming; you really do not want to do that again.

I guess I could have just quit, and walked away with a Master's degree, but in biology, there's not much you can do with that. You can't really teach. If you go to a pharmaceutical company, you only qualify for a mid-level job. If you ever want to move up you'll need to get a PhD eventually, so it's a temporary solution. I remember being so unhappy, I'd go home for Christmas and tell my parents I didn't need to finish; that I hated it enough to leave. I'd tell them I could always go work for the pharmaceutical industry or teach high school. They weren't particularly supportive. But I was so miserable; I didn't really care what I did. I just didn't want to keep doing what I was doing.

At this point, people were leaving the lab left and right. Our postdoc went back to Europe; the other grad student left without finishing her degree. I was searching for a postdoc on the sly. I sent out letters without telling my advisor. Some people, knowing where I was coming from, knew better than to contact him for a reference; others invited me for interviews without the reference. Some contacted my advisor and then I never heard from them again.

I missed out on some great opportunities, including a few that I was really excited about—but by then I'd started to realize that I didn't want to be a professor. I'd seen so many people crumble and die as assistant professors, and I think that reality was starting to sink in. The success rate of junior faculty is so low and it just rips people apart. That wasn't the vision of academia I grew up with, but it was the reality that I was learning from first-hand experience.

By the time I started writing my dissertation, my relationship with my advisor was no longer functional; he'd read a draft and completely disagreed with the content of my paper. My chair, on the other hand, thought it was fine, so he stepped in to fill the role of supervisor while I finished writing. I had a due date coming up, so I stayed home for four weeks straight. I got up every morning and wrote, and watched Passport to Europe on the Travel Channel for an hour at lunch, then I'd write some more, then I had an hour-long break for dinner, and then I'd write until nine or ten at night. I'd call my boyfriend who was living in Europe at the time to talk for a while, then stay up and watch television until I fell asleep. The next day I'd do it all over again. The night before it was due, my roommate and I made a 4:30 a.m. run to Kinko's and Krispy Kreme, and then turned the dissertation in to my committee.

By then I had solved my job problem for at least a year—I accepted a postdoc with one of my committee members because I couldn't get a job with anyone else—and that lifted some of the pressure. Of course the dissertation defense itself was outrageously stressful because there was so much potential for things to go horribly wrong—what with my ex-advisor, my family, and interested members of the public in the audience. I guess I should have been relieved afterward, but the night that I finished the public defense I had a nervous breakdown. I was crying frantically, just shaking, uncontrollably. I'd finished, but all I could think was "I don't want to do anything. I never want to do biology again, I never want to do research again, and I never want to spend time in a lab again." I had a postdoc lined up, but I didn't want to do it. I never, ever, wanted to step foot in a university ever again.

Moving On

A year is actually a very short time to try and line up your next job. So I had a week of "Ahhhh," and then it was like, "Oh shit, I need to figure something out."

It turned out that I could have stayed in that lab beyond the first year; I could have stayed for five years, which would have been a longer-term solution to the job issue. But the director of the lab really wanted her team to put in 14-hour days. After going a hundred miles an hour, a hundred hours a week in my last lab and getting nothing back, I didn't have anything left. The best night's sleep I've ever had was the night after I said "no" to extending the postdoc. I went to my last day of work at the lab, turned in all my keys, came home and passed out asleep, and the idea that I never had to go back to that lab—to any lab, anywhere—that I was free to choose anything else I wanted to do in life was just like, "Ahhhh..." That's the first deep breath I've taken since I was eighteen. Of course, leaving essentially meant burning my academic bridges, but I didn't care that I was taking a one-way exit. I was so happy I would have welded the door shut on the other side.

I moved to Boston—newly single, no roommates, and no job prospects in sight. I had a hard time just getting an apartment because everyone wants to know who your employer is, and of course, I didn't have one. I picked Boston because I liked the city, and it had all of the job possibilities I was considering: pharmaceuticals, publishing, teaching at a small college, or consulting. It also had a great music scene; I joined four orchestras immediately and got into one that was semiprofessional. At that point I almost didn't care if I ever got a job. At least I could play music again. I didn't think I'd stay unemployed for very long, but about six months in, my savings were going really fast. I was doing some freelance science writing, and my parents were contributing too, which I hated. They were trying to be supportive—emotionally as well as financially—but they still thought that going back to academic science was the answer. But you can't just go back.

By then, in addition to everything else, I'd developed an aversion to doing experiments on animals. I remember in undergrad the lab director next door said, "I have a gift for you. It's a 'happy applying for grad school gift.'" He said, "You need to see this before you pick a career." He had a cloth over something and he pulled it off and it was a mouse cage. He said, "Snap its neck." I said, "Do what!?" And he said, "Snap its neck with your bare hands. You want to be a neuroscientist. Tissue has to be fresh. That's the way it happens, kiddo. You have to be good at it because, otherwise, the animal suffers. I'll do one, you do the second one, we'll go for a drink, then you can apply to grad schools." It's true. You grab the poor little thing by the tail, pinch the back of its neck so its spinal cord is stabilized, snap the spinal cord really fast, and it's instantly dead. I did it and nearly passed out. "Well," the lab director said, "one down, 10,000 to go." I was horrified, but I really wanted to do neuroscience. I thought I could do it.

I should have known better. Even though I did it for years and years, I did it every single day. I should have known on my first graduate rotation when I had to go out into the parking lot and cry. I had pets all through grad school, and every time I had a big lab day where I had to kill an entire litter of baby mice all at once, I'd drive through PETCO on the way home and buy a toy for my guinea pig or my cat to try to balance out the karma. It just weighed down on me. I'd go into work some days and there was blood just pouring down the sink. Someone needs to do it because eventually, hopefully, it will lead to saving human lives. I just, personally, couldn't do it anymore.

So I couldn't go back and I wasn't moving forward. Editing and science writing weren't panning out. Money was dwindling, and my parents were pissed off and exasperated. But ironically, the fact that I spent all of my unemployed free time doing music got me the job I have now. One of the girls in my orchestra, who was also a cellist, was a patent attorney. She'd been doing a chemistry PhD, and it was just painful. She went to the career center and realized that she could get the job she wanted without finishing her PhD, so she quit, applied to law firms, got her job, went to law school, and never looked back. I remember it was the first time in a long time that I'd felt genuinely excited about a career prospect.

Still, it took me a while to commit to the idea because going back to school for four more years after the hell I'd just been through was pretty overwhelming. I did the math on how long it would take to do law school at night, exactly which years of my life it would take, and what that meant for potentially meeting someone and starting a family. But eventually I realized that this really did sound like the perfect career for me. Once I decided to make a go of it, everything happened really fast—it was only about a week and a half from when I interviewed to when I got the offer.

Turns out, what I'm doing is all part of a well-trod career path—I just never knew anything about it until my friend from orchestra told me. No one at my grad school ever acknowledged that there was any kind of legitimate career for a PhD scientist beyond academia. Admittedly, it's probably not for everyone. Getting a PhD is harrowing enough; following that up with four more years that are completely focused on work and school is crazy. But there's a good payoff at the end. A good career, a solid salary, and the possibility of work/life balance.

My dad wasn't convinced until he went to a bunch of conferences and started talking to other scientists. "My crazy daughter has a science PhD, but she signed up for law school, and she thinks she's going to be a patent attorney." All of his colleagues were like, "Oh, that's fabulous; you have no idea. My kid's doing that too." Then my dad says, "Yeah, did I say crazy? I meant fabulous." After about six months of running my decision past people he respected in his academic circles, and finding out that a bunch of their kids with MDs and PhDs were doing the same, he came around; he was ready to say, "Okay, it's a good choice."

It *was* a good choice; this is the perfect career for me. I only wish I'd known about it earlier. The vision I had as a kid of a professor's day-to-day work and lifestyle just wasn't in line with the reality of academic scientists, especially at junior stages. It was in line with someone of my dad's generation, working in a different field at a different kind of university. I still love science, and I'm happy to say that grad school didn't kill that love. But I absolutely do not love working on animals, and I don't love bench work—which are two very separate things from not loving science. I feel like I would have ended up doing something nonacademic with my PhD eventually, regardless; I don't feel like I was driven here by evil people or bad experiences. I like the fact that, in the end, what makes me happy, and what makes my parents happy for me, involved jumping off the path that had been laid out for me. I don't have to wake up and worry, "Did I do this because I was trained, subconsciously, from an early age, to think this is what I wanted to do?" I think if I had stayed in academia that doubt would have always been in the back of my head.

This career has allowed me to build a really good life, one that includes music. I earn enough money to live in a great city where I can play in a professional orchestra in my free time. I can buy an amazing cello if I want. I can buy season tickets to the Boston Symphony anytime I want. This career enables a major music hobby, and keeps it fun. I had an accompanist once who was an incredibly accomplished pianist. He told me, "If you love it, don't make it your career. Every time you don't make an orchestra or you don't get the job or you don't get the solo or whatever, you'll resent it a little bit more." I understand what he was saying on a different level now. Even though it still bothers me sometimes that the choice not to pursue a music career was made for me, I don't regret it. I feel like I get the best of both worlds. I finally know what I'm going to do when I grow up, and I have music back.

Interview: Peter Weller

PhD, Art History

Actor: *Robocop, Naked Lunch, Star Trek Into Darkness, Dexter, 24* (among others)

Director: *Sons of Anarchy, Hawaii Five-O, House* (among others)

What is it like to be a famous actor, and a graduate student, at the same time?

I was directing a show for A&E called "Longmire" and they'd given me the day off to present my dissertation to my committee. So that day I got up and went to work, then got on a plane to LA. Paramount, thank god, gave me a limo to get from the airport to campus, so I came to UCLA and did my hour-long presentation. I'm talking to a hundred historians, art historians, some Italians, and so forth. My friends from the Getty Museum were there, all of my medievalist scholar friends, a couple of people from Florence. I talked a mile a minute. It was thrilling. At the end, I asked if there were any questions and at first there was silence, but then one of my advisors asked a question, then another person asked a question. I'm starting to hold court and I see my wife at the back of the room—she's running her hand past her neck, signaling me to "kill it," like, the more you talk the more they're going to get on you, man! You know how art historians are. I cut it off after five minutes. Got back in the limo. Went to the opening of *Star Trek Into Darkness*, went to the party afterward, and discoed until four o'clock in the morning with the cast of *Star Trek*. Got back on the plane for another hour, and was at work the next day at six o'clock. I stayed up a whole 24 hours and I was never running on empty. It was on a Thursday, thank god, so that Friday night I slept like a baby. That was an unbelievable day—one of the most exciting days I've ever had.

Where are you with your dissertation?

I'm turning it in to my committee in 14 days, and then the committee is going to read, I don't know, 500 pages of text and 29 pages of appendices and 67 pages of footnotes, and look at 170 images. Are they actually going to read all that? I don't know. I'm hoping they'll just sign off on it and say, yeah, file it. I've been working on the dissertation for two full years, maybe a little longer. This thing is a tome. My wife says, "Who in the hell is going to read that?" And I think well, somebody will at some point, hopefully.

How long have you been in grad school?

I've been doing graduate work for 15 years—since my first class in 1998. When I started taking classes I didn't intend to earn even a master's degree, but I kept with it and got the master's degree a few years later. I did the walk in Florence and everything at Syracuse University. I didn't intend to get a PhD right away. Then around 2006 I found out there was some regulation that said you could only use letters of recommendations for three years or something like that. The guys who were going to recommend me—I don't want to say were really old, but they were in their sixties and seventies and eighties and I thought, well, I can't get these recommendations and just hold on to them, they may be dead when I decide to get a PhD. I might as well apply for it now. I applied and was accepted at UCLA and NYU. I didn't want to go back to New York so I stayed here. And the rest is art history.

You work on Renaissance art, right?

Renaissance art, intellectual history; it's an interdisciplinary thing. My dissertation is on the intellectual and visual sources that would have informed Leon Battista Alberti and his book *De Pictura*, before he ever hit Florence in 1434. It's been a cliché for a very long time that Alberti ended up in Florence in 1434, saw Masaccio, Donatello, Ghiberti, wrote a book, *De Pictura*, and became a genius. My whole argument is that his education, his sensibilities, his entire proclivity for art, design, the visual medium, and intellectual antique history started way before Florence. He did not get to Florence, see Donatello and Ghiberti, and go wow, I'm going to write a book on art, and I'm going to do it in the form of Quintilian's Institutio Oratoria, and it's going to blow minds—all in one year. That is so much horseshit. So my topic is Alberti before Florence, the sources informing *De Pictura*.

What prompted you—a successful actor—to pursue a PhD?

My father had a degree in history, and my brother is very bright, my uncles are all very bright. My cousins are all summa cum laude guys and I was probably trying to keep up with them. I'd really point toward my father because he instilled a fascination

with history in me. And then, if you like movies, how can you
not like painting? I was actually inspired to go look at medieval
Italian art by a well-known, award-winning director of photog-
raphy named Vittorio Storaro who won Oscars for *Apocalypse
Now* and a few other films of note. I was at a film festival in
Japan in the early 1990s talking about ancient Rome with
Vittorio and he asked, "Peter, have you ever been to Padua?
Have you ever seen Giotto in the Cappella Scrovegni, the Arena
Chapel in Padua?" That fresco is the first movie ever made in
the Western world. It's the first real emotional narrative visual
discourse; the entire story of Mary and Jesus. But at the time I
was speaking with Vittorio I had not seen it. Vittorio is a genius,
and he's all dressed up in his Versace and whatever and he said,
"Peter, we cannot discuss art until you see Giotto in Padua."
And he walked away. So I went to see Giotto in Padua in the
days when you could have a cup of coffee and smoke a cigar in
the place and stay in there for hours, freezing at Christmas time,
and the frescoe cycle, of course, blew my mind. My dissertation
is on Padua, essentially.

**Where were you in your film career when you made the deci-
sion to get a graduate degree?**

I was quite successful; I mean, I made a good living at it. I'd
finished a movie and was about to start another, and I decided
to jump over to Italy and take a course with the head of the
department at Syracuse. After that course he said, you might
want to take another couple of courses and see about this master's degree program in Florence. So I applied to the program
and was accepted, but kept postponing. After three years they
said, you've got to do it, or not do it. That coincided with a
union shutdown in my industry so I went off and did the program in Florence.

I thought, I'll just go over there and hike to class, live in Florence, and then on weekends go down to my place on the Amalfi Coast and groove. When I got there, I was informed that I didn't have any undergraduate courses in art history at all and was strongly advised to audit them. So I'm up hiking to school at seven o'clock in the morning with 20 year olds and I'm in classes all morning long, and then teaching in the afternoon. That's one of the reasons the Syracuse program is so rigorous—you have to teach. "By the way, here's a class of fifty kids; take them to Assisi, teach them Simone Martini in the lower church of Assisi." I'd never been to Assisi. I get on the train, I go two days ahead of time to look at this thing. You can study that stuff until the cows come home, but you ain't ready in 48 hours to teach it to kids.

The beautiful thing about being in Florence is that you're literally in front of the art that everyone has talked about for 800 years. You're working with German, French, and Italian scholars, and with Latin. Some of the seminal scholars in art history are coming in and guest lecturing. It's really PhD-level work. As difficult as my PhD at UCLA is, it is a cakewalk compared to a master's degree in Florence. Don't get me wrong; the PhD, particularly the dissertation, is an ocean of writing. However, in Florence I had to take paleography, then attend lectures in archives—reading antique text and medieval text. I didn't know enough Latin and I didn't know enough medieval scholarship to get my head around it. It killed me. I was about to quit after a month.

Florence can bust you; it's a beautiful city to visit but not the easiest place in which to live. It's very small, claustrophobic, extraordinarily humid. Mosquitoes in the winter time, the river is not friendly. The city has some of the all-time crap food you've ever eaten in your life. I've had better Italian food than that in New Jersey. So I was going to quit. I said,

I'm a made guy, why am I walking to school in this hellhole of tourism? But then my mother and my wife came over and said, you don't quit anything, so why are you going to quit this? So I stayed, and I taught, and at the end of the first semester I was packing my bags in the car, with no intention of returning in the fall; and there was a note from one of my professors, saying that he wanted to see me. And my professor said, "I want you to be my teaching assistant next fall." And I said, "Man, you've got seven other students here who are from Rutgers, Brown, Harvard, Yale, University of Michigan; I'm the caboose at the end of your train. Why in the heck do you want me to do it?" And he said, "Because you've been in front of the art longer; and you teach it from a point of view of relevant visual media—the movies. Kids watch movies. And kids listen to you."

By the time I got to UCLA my mind was open on another level; I'd been trying to get there in Florence but I was so over-whelmed by it all. A third of all of the Western world's art before the twentieth century is in Italy, and a third of that third is in Florence. It's Stendhal syndrome; the depression that Florence brings on is not a fiction. You've got a guy in his fifties who goes over there and he thinks he's going to get a master's degree in art and he has to teach that stuff day and night and write papers on it and do hour-long presentations in front of it—it's a killer. Some people say it's easy. I found it backbreaking.

Which has been more challenging, course work and exams, or the dissertation?

I don't want to say that course work is easier, but it's more mea-sured because you have to go to class and you have to take notes. The regimen of it is laid out for you. The written exams were really challenging; at seven o'clock in the morning on a

Monday, you get a ding on your computer and they give you the subjects and you have one week to write. My wife was gone out on a job on the road so I got up every morning, and I wrote for nine or ten hours a day for seven days, and I cooked popcorn, pasta, and bean soup out of the same pot that whole time. That was actually fun—like climbing Mt. Everest. Nobody but you there, lock the doors. I kind of wish the dissertation was like that.

How has that been, the writing process?

I feel overwhelmed by this dissertation. I mean I don't know anybody that's written a dissertation that doesn't feel overwhelmed by it. I've got 40 more books to go through, 40 more sources I want to tap into. And my wife says, "When are you going to end this?" And I say, "When I do these 40 more sources." She says, "Don't you have to turn it in?" I say "Yeah, I don't know how I'm going to do it." My cousin's wife has a PhD in sociology. She says, "I'll tell you how to do it, write 'the *fucking* end.' That's how you do it." And you know what, she's right. In my office I've still got 40 secondary sources that lead to primary sources. But I'm cooked. Maybe it was the e-mail from UCLA saying turn this in or you're gone. Finally you start to edit and you say, yeah I want this done now. Someday I want to turn this into a book, do the teaching and all that. But I want this part of it, this endless footnoting of the same damn thing, to be over.

Has it been a challenge to merge two different, very intense, careers?

The fortunate thing is that course work and exams coincided with a particular shift in my career, where I was moving into directing television and being very selective about my projects. So I had a lot of time for grad school. By the time the dissertation started rolling around I was getting a lot of directing gigs. The writing phase is when I really had to meld the career with the dissertation because I work all summer long. I do the dissertation on the weekends. I took a vacation with my wife to Prague and Paris and Venice, and I was writing on the train. It haunts you. The book *Writing Your Dissertation in Fifteen Minutes a Day* was life changing. Get up and write it in the morning. Commit to 15 minutes a day and that will turn into an hour and that's all you've got to do. That "eight hours on a Friday" method just doesn't work.

What about balancing the final throes of writing with family commitments?

I have a two-year-old now, and it's scary, because he'll come up and start punching computer buttons right in the middle of my dissertation. I mean, I looked at one of my folders the other day, and it had no label on it anymore. I opened it up and it was the edits of the first draft, but what happened to the title? My wife says, "Teddy got on to your computer." I went, "Listen, Teddy cannot get on to the damn computer! My dissertation is going to turn into ABCmouse in a second!" Yeah, I've seen the stress of grad school really take a toll on some marriages. My wife has been really good about it. She's an old soul, a really great woman, but she has her limits. She says, "I want this done. Get that thing done." She doesn't allow any Latin in the bedroom, no Latin books in the bedroom. We were on vacation and I had this Latin text with me; she says, "Take that damn thing out of here, man." I say, "It's a hotel room." "I don't care," she says; "It ain't coming in this bedroom." I have to tell you, I'm submitting in two weeks but I don't really believe it. It's like getting out of jail. Or more like, they're saying this is when you're going to be released and you kind of won't believe it until it happens. Can I really turn this thing in? I'm crossing my fingers that they won't red ink the thing too much.

If you get out of jail, how's life going to change for you?

All I can think about is the joy of turning this thing in, and the huge weight that's going to lift, and then somebody saying, okay, you're a doctor now. My dearest friend—he's an antiquarian book dealer—he says, "You'll feel great for about a week, but knowing you, you'll find another Everest to climb." So it will be like that. But what the hell, you've got to do it all. I've been asked by UCLA to teach a film directing class in their film department. And there's a classics film history class that I want to teach that I taught at Syracuse called, "Hollywood and the Roman Empire." So I've got that syllabus to do. I love presenting papers—the Renaissance Society, the Sixteenth Century Society. I want to publish another couple of articles, and publish this book. I've got to remember, like my advisor says, the dissertation is not the book. This is just a draft; stop trying to make it perfect. Yeah, turning a dissertation into a book—that's a whole other nightmare.

Can you see your two careers merging gracefully in the future?

I certainly hope so. I'm a spiritual guy and I leave a lot of it to God. It may not look harmonious but everybody else says wow, how can you do all this—I also play jazz—and have a kid? You just do it; you schedule it. You get up in the morning. You've got your hour and a half with your kid before he goes to toddler school. Play the trumpet for an hour. Do the dissertation for an hour or two. Certain days you've got to work, like, 18 hours so you can't do the dissertation then. Other days the workload is light so you take the thing and work on it during the down time. Leonardo da Vinci, there's a workaholic for you; the thing that got him through everything was curiosity. And if you have curiosity then you'll go do this stuff. There's a point in your fifties where you just start doing the things that inspire you; all the stuff you didn't do in your twenties and thirties and forties and said I'll do it later. In your fifties you start doing it, and god forbid if you don't because then you'll be living with regret. Now, every life's got a little bit of disappointment. I don't mind the disappointment. I just don't want the regret.

What do you know now that you wish you'd known at the start of it all?

A great intellectual historian at UCLA told me you have to write as you read. Don't be one of those guys who thinks he's going to underline stuff as he goes along, keep doing all this reading, and then at the end he's going to sit at the computer and type up his notes. You've forgotten it all by then. Whenever you have a flash of insight, of inspiration, like the summation of something you've been thinking about, write it down. Don't think you're going to remember it—get it into the computer. You'll see it all starts to fall into shape. Then you edit it and you pull it into your argument.

Here's another thing. There's a great screenwriting boot camp that I attended 20 years ago that said it. The book I mentioned, *Writing Your Dissertation in Fifteen Minutes a Day*, repeats it. Every writer I've ever talked to says it—Gore Vidal, Saul Bellow. Make writing a priority. Hit it in the morning before the detours of daily living get in your way. Even if you have writer's block, write garbage. Sit your ass in the chair because you can't save it for a rainy day. I'm a procrastinator; as much as I get done in a day I'd still rather play with my kid, play golf, hang out—do anything else. So you've got to do it first. You can write your way into thinking, but you cannot think your way into writing.

Interview: Karen Kelsky
Former Tenured Professor
Founder, *The Professor is In*

Did you always know you wanted to be a professor?

I was one of those people who was practically born knowing that I wanted to be a professor. I grew up in Pittsburgh and my father, who was a doctor, had an office down in Oakland where the University of Pittsburgh is located. When I would visit him at his office, I would always go to the Pitt campus—Carnegie Mellon is also down there—and I adored it. I said, this is for me; I love books, I'm a book worm. As soon as I figured out what a professor was, I knew that's what I had been born to do. I always felt really lucky about that, because I watched friends who struggled more in figuring out their calling. I always knew mine, and it was consistent—even though I did, in fact, drop out of two separate graduate programs.

Were there any bumps in the road?

I dropped out of a program at Michigan in public policy and I dropped out of a program at Johns Hopkins in the international studies realm; finally I realized that I wanted to go into a traditional humanities field and once I figured that out, I started a PhD. Initially I wanted to do a PhD in postwar American literature, specifically the beatnik authors. But when

I read the beatnik authors they were all writing about Zen Buddhism, which led me to the study of Japan, and eventually Japan became my area within the field of cultural anthropology. It seems like a big change, but there was a logic to it. I had a lot of struggles throughout the process, but I never doubted that it was the right thing to do. And then, I struggled badly on the job market but never doubted that academia was the career I was supposed to have. Then I got the job and got tenure, then got a better job, and continued to feel that I was absolutely on the right path.

Why did you leave academia?

So there I was: tenured, department head, ensconced in a big ten institution, earning extremely good money. I had a good life, two kids, a nice house. But then I ended up in a really dreadful divorce and custody battle that extended over seven years. Throughout that time all of my energies went toward protecting my children, and the energy that didn't go toward that went toward being an administrator—a department head—and the energy that didn't go toward those two things went to being utterly and completely miserable. I was at the University of Illinois, and completely ill-suited for that kind of environment. I should never have gone to a university like that—I didn't know how good I had it at Oregon. It was a bad mistake. Someone else could have reversed it; could have gone back on the job market and gotten back to Oregon or another West Coast school, and just pretended like it had never happened. But because of my custody situation and my ex-husband, the lawyers told me I couldn't leave until the children were 18, and they were, like, eight at the time. Unless—they said—my partner of ten years at that point would get a full-time job back in Oregon, and I would commit to being a stay-at-home mom. The courts are traditional, and the only way they would consider the move to be in the best interests of the children, is if I made that commitment. So that's what we did. My partner got a job, we went to court, I committed to being a full-time stay-at-home mother—and we won our case. It was path breaking. Even straight couples almost never win those kinds of cases, and we were gay.

You mention being ill-suited for Illinois; how important are quality of life issues in an academic career?

When I was on the market the first time out of my PhD I was a finalist for two positions, one at Oregon and one at Stanford. I ended up with the position at Oregon and it took me years to get over the disappointment. But about five years into my job there I realized how tremendously lucky I was. The people at Oregon were really willing to combine a personal life with their work life which made it a delightful place, and I didn't know how unusual it was until I left—I assumed all campuses were like that. Now, of course, I know that if I'd gone to Stanford I would have been dreadfully unhappy. And I know that because I went to Illinois, where I was dreadfully unhappy, because people won't acknowledge the importance of the personal within a professional context. There is no time clock. You don't punch in, you don't punch out. You are literally never off the clock. You wake up in the morning, and you go to bed at night, with the sense of, oh, my god, what have I not gotten done? It's the article, or the book, or the conference paper, or the lecture. It's a very painful way to live. We put this pressure on ourselves, and there are literally no boundaries. You have to create your own boundaries and maintain them with vigilance—and that includes a true commitment to your family and your mental health and a reasonable work/life balance. I don't think this was a problem for professors 50, or 40, or maybe even 30 years ago; I think they could have kids and coach their softball teams.

But we don't have off switches anymore because of our newer productivity-oriented neoliberal downsizing ethos—unless we really commit to it on a personal level.

How often do you hear this from clients, that they have jobs that look good on paper, but aren't tenable for lifestyle reasons, and so they're back on the job market?

Practically everybody who comes to me for help with a second job has concerns in this area. Everyone's story is unique, of course, and yet they're all similar: they don't feel supported, they don't have the right resources for their research, the expectations are exhausting, the isolation, the loneliness, the alienation—some combination of all of those things. What I always worry about—and I never actually say this to any client because it's impossible to say—I worry that they're not going to find a better situation somewhere else. I always, absolutely, encourage them to try because I mean, it's like being in a bad marriage—you should never stay in a bad marriage just because you think you won't find anything better. Of course you have to make a change. But jobs right now in the academy are not pretty. And a lot of people end up making peace with their current situation, and perhaps reducing their expectations of a perfect fit to some extent. You realize, I have a job, health insurance, benefits, a retirement plan, and the teaching load isn't too bad and now I have three children. How are we going to make this work?

On the subject of making it work, what are some of the pros and cons of leaving academia for entrepreneurship?

I could write a book on this. In fact, I want to. Academics often think of themselves as risk-takers and radicals and fearless fighters, when in fact, as a group, they are incredibly conservative, risk averse, fearful, hypercautious, and insecure. Those are qualities that mitigate 100 percent against being entrepreneurial. It took me a few steps to transition from being a typical academic to being someone who could launch my own business. The first step was becoming a department head, because in that role I had to deal with money. I had to handle it and fight for it; I began to feel comfortable talking about money and gained confidence with balancing budgets. Humanities professors—probably academics as a whole outside of business schools—we're trained to feel that we are above money. But as a department head I learned that understanding money is really important; you need to know where it comes from and where it goes.

The second step was when I started to run my own small business. Before I left my last university I was completely miserable and trying to find an outlet. I'm an artistic person, so I started making jewelry and crafts out of my collection of Japanese paper and selling them from a card table in a parking lot at the Saturday farmer's market. I loved it. I was like, wow, I can make stuff with my own hands and people will pay me for it; how cool is that? It was so gratifying. So much better than whatever that weird shit is that we do in academia where you produce, like, nothing; you produce words and abstractions. You never know who reads them, and you teach students stuff that they don't want to learn; I mean, it's crazy.

When I needed to find a way to make money after I'd left the university, I thought about starting *The Professor is In* and I wasn't afraid to try because I knew how to handle money, and I had already run a business, and I knew I had a skill that was potentially useful. I didn't know if I would be successful, but I knew that it was at least a plausible business idea. I'd already made a simple website for my jewelry business and so I just did it; I just threw another website together and put it out there.

And boom—it hit; it took off right away. I had my first client within about five days and more clients quickly after that. I wrote an article for the *Chronicle of Higher Education* about my new business and they let me use my real name. It's called "Memo to Professors" and starts, "Dear Professors, I advise your students for money. Why do I do it? Because you don't..." and then it goes on from there. After that came out, hundreds and hundreds of people got in touch with me and it's been like that ever since. It's been three years, and I've worked with at least 2,000 clients at this point.

What advice would you give your former self, if you could?

Academia is a cult. You're socialized into the cult and you believe there are no value systems outside of it. The alleged point of graduate school is to train you, and help you write a dissertation, but the underlying agenda is to bring you into the cult so that you don't question its premises or its value system, and you live according to them yourself. All of the suffering we're seeing now is the result of that system having an economic meltdown. It's not sustainable anymore, because there aren't enough jobs for all of those indoctrinated cult members. You have to leave the cult in order to survive, but it's not easy to leave. No one knows how. What I wish I could say to my former self, and what I do say emphatically to my readers and clients, is don't drink the Kool-Aid. Academia can provide a good job and a fine career. Absolutely try to do it, but understand that the work is very hard, and the system—with all of its expectations—is rigid. You're going to have to follow the rules. But you don't have to believe *ipso facto* that there are no other things of value in the world. You can do something else. It is okay to quit. I give you permission. You have not failed. You can still hold your head up. There are other ways to live.

I think sometimes what holds people back is the fear of losing their community—and the sense that it's a one-way exit.

The people who leave will lose many friends, it's true. But they likely won't lose all of their friends, and they will make new ones. I think we're in a time of real transition; three years ago when I would run into faculty, they would sort of smirk, or quickly brush me off at the party and go talk to someone important, right? Now, when I'm talking with tenured faculty—the people most invested in this system—they hear about my job and their eyes light up and they're like, "Wait a minute. You do what? So how's it work?" In the last three years the situation has become so much more awful and desperate that even faculty members are coming to acknowledge that it's a crisis. Many people are making other choices, and this is something worth thinking and talking about. So, I think the social isolation is in flux. People who leave will lose some of their highly indoctrinated friends, because the act of leaving casts doubt upon their cult beliefs. But there will be new friends, and different friends—and old friends who will surprise you.

In terms of the one-way thing, yeah, it is one way. Even when there were more jobs, it wasn't easy to leave academia and then come back. Now that there are so few jobs, I don't see anyone who leaves being able to come back easily. The competition is so intense. If you're gone for three years doing some alternative academic job or some library job, a curator job, and you try to get back in, you're now competing not just with your cohort and the people ahead of you but also with the people from the three years behind you—everyone who's been active in the system during those years when you probably weren't publishing. That being said, my clients surprise me. I work with people who have pretty nontraditional records, and I don't think they're going to be able to find a tenure-track academic job. But sometimes they do. So don't rush to judgment about your record because your assessment may well be inaccurate. Have your record studied by somebody who can give you a reality check as to whether you really are as bad off as you think you are.

It sounds like you never lost your love of academia, or your sense that it was your path. If circumstances were to change, is it something that you would consider going back to?

You know, it's so funny; just the other day someone I know from the academy told me there was a position opening up that might be a possibility for me. I had literally never entertained that possibility and the reason, of course, is that I don't publish and I don't do research, I don't do writing, I'm not teaching so I have no record. So how could I possibly get hired? It would be contrary to everything I've ever written on my own blog! But in any case, it really floored me to think about the possibility of going back into the academy and I was like, wow, would I do it? To tell you the truth, I think that my passion for the academy, the fact that I love it as deeply as I do, is why my blog is popular and my business is successful. I think people trust me. They know that I get it, and I'm not bitter. Academia is a pretty cool career and yet, I really don't have a ton of desire to go back into it. I don't miss the teaching or the meetings. What else is there? I don't miss the research, or the imperative to write, or the academic conferences. I do miss having colleagues who are smart and witty and engaged and just down the hall that I could go have coffee with. But you know what? That's not a good enough reason to go back into a career.

Where are your career aspirations these days; where would you like to be in five years?

I was supposed to have written the first *The Professor is In* book this summer and like every other academic, I can't get my damn book done. Oh, my god. I'm here again. Just where I thought I wouldn't be! In five years I would like to have two or three *The Professor is In* books done, because as much as we all love blogs and the Internet, there is no substitute for a book on your shelf that you can refer to when you have a question. One of my subspecialties is women and the ways that women sabotage themselves through gendered habits that are inculcated by society; I'd like to do more writing and speaking on women's self-expression more generally—beyond the academy. I'd like to bring some employees on board to help with my business so that I can spend more time writing and speaking. And I have a great desire to go around the country, speaking to groups. I think I'm good at it and I love to teach, and it's very gratifying work. But I still have two kids at home who are twelve and fourteen, and it's pretty disruptive for me to leave town. So I'm saving the jet-setting stage of the career for about five years from now.

Sidebar 2: What I Know Now That I Wish I Knew Then

"When you're feeling stuck, just remember, no one will ever read your dissertation."

"I wish I had avoided including professors on my dissertation committee that I knew weren't the biggest fans of my work. I thought I had to have certain big names on the committee to be taken seriously on the job market. BIG MISTAKE."

"If your advisor is difficult to work with and/or doesn't value your project, change your advisor rather than trying to change yourself. It's a tough move, but it is way more difficult to lie about who you are, or to tolerate years of abuse."

"Never ever try to reinvent the wheel. The process may be fun, but in the end it won't advance your project at all."

"Outsource as much as you can (there are other people who do that task better than you ever could) and don't be afraid to go get temporary training elsewhere. One month in another lab is better than six months struggling by yourself."

"If a project doesn't work, start something else. The deeper you get into an unproductive project, the more difficult it is to change it."

"Go where the data is taking you. If the committee is reasonable, you'll graduate if you did solid work, even if you changed the main focus."

"Before I left on my big research trip, I was feeling a lot of anxiety about how to make the trip productive and get to every archive, artist, etc. A junior faculty member told me to stop stressing—that I'd write about whatever I found. Turns out, she was right. That was exactly what I did."

"I wish I'd known that I would probably never again have the time to focus so intensely on my own research, and to write and revise and write and revise. I've used various parts of my dissertation for subsequent publications—and it turns out, it was pretty good writing! So it pays to take the time to do all of those revisions."

"I wish I had known that you don't need to dedicate your life to the dissertation, you just have to dedicate daily time to it, even a half an hour a day. It is all about nurturing that daily relationship and much less about full time dedication."

"NO ONE READS YOUR DISSERTATION!!! No, seriously, no one reads it. Remember that when you're agonizing over the details."

"Use all of your committee members when you need help; your chair is the most important certainly, but not necessarily the one you need at each step along the way. Any support is good support."

"Anything that takes six to ten years to complete has a lot of time built in for course-correction. There's time to take risks, make some mistakes, and try out a few different paths."

"Living in a perpetual state of anxiety can, eventually, rewire your brain in a permanent way. Don't think that you'll 'bounce back' to being your pre-grad school self once the dissertation is over; some of the cognitive and emotional habits you cultivate will be there to stay—for better, or for worse."

"Advice to students' partners: Take it seriously, but find some emotional distance too; there are a lot of highs and lows in academia that you can support someone through, without needing to feel them as well."

"Life is life. In grad school or out, whether on the tenure track or off, you can't escape yourself."

Part III

PhDs Redirected

Chapter 7

Rodrigo
Graduate Work in American Studies
Registered Nurse

One of the biggest things I learned from grad school was that just because I can do something doesn't mean I should be doing it . . .

Getting There

Graduate school was an idea that came from my undergraduate mentors. They thought that I had an interesting voice and as a student of color, some interesting perspectives, and could potentially be a leader. They didn't think I should just let it all go when I finished my undergraduate program. Honestly, I had other aspirations at the time and I was kind of skeptical. Not about whether or not I could do the work, I just wasn't sure if I *should* be doing that work. It ended up being kind of a crapshoot. I wasn't sure that I'd get into any of the schools my mentors were recommending, but thought I'd apply and see what happened. I wasn't sure where my music career was going or what I wanted to do next. I wasn't sure if I should keep trying to "make it" or if I should take academia off the back burner and see where it might go. To my dismay, I got a lot of acceptance letters, and they were offering me money. I decided, maybe this wasn't in my thoughts until recently, but maybe I need to give it a shot. Then I decided, if I'm going to do this then I'm really going to do this. You think I have the goods, let me see if I have the goods. The desire and the motivation were both kind of a conscious decision, and it all came together right when I started grad school.

I was 29 years old at the time, and had been pursuing a career in music for a while. The year before I started grad school I was still thinking about how to make it as a rock star, and thinking about going on tour. I was developing some momentum, playing pretty regularly in blues clubs in New York. It was fun, and I was working with good people, musically. There weren't a lot of blues venues, though, so I wasn't working nearly as much as I would have liked, and I was having to think about whether or not New York was the best place for me, music-wise. At the time, I was involved in a serious relationship that kind of complicated things because I wasn't quite sure my partner would want to go on tour with me, or would accept the life that going on tour entailed. But I didn't have a record deal or anything like that, yet. If I had been offered a record deal, I don't think that graduate school would have been an option for me. I definitely would have gone ahead and seen that part of my life through to its logical conclusion.

Since I didn't really have anything solid lined up, graduate school sounded like a pretty good choice. Trying to make it as a musician can involve a lot of poverty, which I was familiar with, and grad school seemed like a better choice in that way too—and like it might allow me, somewhere down the line, to get back to music again. But there was a conversation that should have happened before I even applied to graduate school. Someone should have asked me if I wanted to do this for the rest of my life—spend it in libraries and archives, doing research. I'm not sure if I would have opted out, even then, but I would have asked if there was a different way to get to my end goal. My aspirations have never included being a tenured professor with a nice house on the water. I just wanted to teach. There might have been a better way for me to get there from where I was.

Getting Through

From the beginning I knew that I wouldn't be able to pursue both music and academia simultaneously, and as it turns out, I was right. You know how it is, once you're in it, you feel like if you do anything else, you're kind of cheating on your marriage. I had taken a couple years off, so it took a little while to get my momentum back. Probably the bigger transition for me was that I had not lived anywhere outside of New York before—that, and being separated from my friends and family. It was a very isolating experience, and I didn't realize just how much I would miss playing music until I stopped. But a lot of that resolved itself within the first six months. You get so sucked into the work, and all the new things you're seeing, and the new people you're meeting—going to the conferences and reading all these great books. I found a pizzeria that was open relatively late which made it feel a little bit more like New York.

Academically, I found my stride pretty quickly. Jumping into the work and adjusting to the pace, I was always cool with that. Not a big deal. I actually liked writing a lot, so that was helpful. The classes were always filled with really interesting people. The biggest challenge, and this was a continuous theme throughout graduate school, was that I never quite felt like graduate school was a good fit for me. I felt a little out of place. Doing the work was easy enough, I just wasn't sure I was the one who should be doing it. For the first few years I was just kind of cruising, not thinking too far ahead, just trying to get the work done. A lot of that had to do with all the other things that were going on in my life at the time. But I think it was also related to my initial indecision about graduate school in the first place. I always joked that once I finished grad school I would probably do something completely different anyway. That's just typical of me. But maybe it was wish fulfillment, because that's exactly what happened.

I was a little stressed out when it came time to do the qualifying exams; the workload felt about the same, but I didn't like the fact that it wasn't structured. It felt like—okay now everything is on your shoulders: you have to be familiar with this book list, and we're not going to tell you how to do it. But it needs to be done, so I got the work done, obviously. But I definitely had a lot of anxiety for that year not knowing if I was studying appropriately or effectively. I liked the structure of the coursework years and when that ended, it was somewhat maddening for me. I'm actually fairly structured in my life, but I'm better with the short-term goals; I take things more week-by-week. I don't think as much about the longer-term goals and that's because I don't step back from the painting to see the bigger picture until I feel like I've really completed the specific part that I'm focusing on.

When I left New York, my grandmother was still relatively independent; she could perform most of her self-care and was able to get around the house okay. So, I didn't have to be there or call every day, though I usually did. It was only after I started working on my dissertation that things started to go downhill. It wasn't overnight, but gradually I became the go to person regarding her care and decision making. That definitely made focusing on grad school more of a challenge. I needed to spend more and more time with her, and even when I wasn't there, often my mind was. It was difficult to talk about within my grad community. I didn't want anyone to think I was just whining, and I definitely didn't want to hear any "suck it up; man up" speeches. I certainly didn't feel comfortable discussing family responsibilities, and how they were conflicting with grad school, with my advisors. To be fair, they want you to finish—that's their priority. I'm sure they would have tried to help, but it would have been filtered through a larger need to help me finish. But eventually, reality became bigger than my dissertation, and I withdrew from the community—from social activities and stuff like that. I just had too much on my mind. I also felt a little bit older than a lot of my colleagues in the program and like we couldn't really relate to each other. I know some people had kids. But as far as being the primary caretaker for an older family member, I don't think many people had that experience.

The real turning point for me, though, was when I got sick about five years into the program. I wasn't given a very good prognosis at first, so I just stopped working for a while. It was a pleasant surprise when everyone, including my dissertation committee, came to my side and were really supportive, and encouraged me to just focus on getting well, which translated into don't worry about your dissertation right now. It was about four or five months after an initial surgery that the doctors told me things would be okay—though I still needed more time to recover. I'd been planning to move when the health problems started so I was actually between apartments, staying on a friend's couch for a couple of weeks, and had nothing to do but get well and think about what was next. I just couldn't seem to get my batteries charged up again. I worked on my dissertation, so that I'd have material to share with my committee, but it seemed—even to me—like it was half-assed.

Getting sick completely changed my priorities. I realized that writing my dissertation wasn't a pleasant thing to do; it didn't make me happy in any way. And even though I was really interested in the material, I didn't have anything innovative to say about it. Getting deeply engaged in the discourse of your work makes you remarkably boring to everyone who doesn't do the same work, and I already felt separated from my friends; grad school had even dealt a deathblow to the relationship I had when I started because my then-fiancé did not understand why I was so disengaged from everyone, including her. I wanted to reverse that trend, not continue it.

I worked on my dissertation and tried to get back into things for over a year, but at some point, I just knew that I had better start thinking about something else. One of the things that came up, while I was going through the healing process, was that I was really interested in diet, nutrition, and fitness. Thinking and learning about those things made me happy; they were useful for me personally, and I realized that I could use what I knew to help others. As I continued in that direction, grad school became smaller and smaller to me; I didn't want to think about it anymore. The doctors didn't know what caused my illness—I didn't have any previous indications, and they couldn't tell me how to avoid it in the future other than to take better care of myself. I felt that my stress levels were a major contributing factor, and that I needed to manage stress better. At that time, the major stress-inducing factor in my life was grad school. It wasn't feeding me, but in many ways, starving me. So that's when I knew I needed to go. I told myself that at some point, maybe, I could return but for now I needed to let it go. I never had any formal conversations with anyone on my dissertation committee; I just stopped contacting them. I think they kind of knew what was going on.

When I was in grad school, I read a lot about the isolation certain types of students feel in university settings. Much of what I read focused on students of color, and while I didn't necessarily think of myself that way—I've always felt more "gray" than "other"—I did identify with what I was reading, in that there were very few ways in which I could relate to the people all around me, and I'm not sure why. Maybe I'm too much of an artist, or a musician, or too much of a Queens, New Yorker, or my responsibilities are too different, or whatnot, but I did feel very outside and apart from everyone. Once people kind of huddled around me when I got sick, and I started listening to music a lot again, and started playing guitar more, I was like, okay, this is why I felt so weird for so long because I hadn't been doing this—I hadn't been doing the things that sustain me. I'm not a religious person, and I don't believe in fate, but I do think that for whatever reason, getting sick helped me get back on a better path. I think I was hoping for a little help; I was hoping that someone would push me off the treadmill.

Moving On

Things can get really tight, financially, when you're in graduate school. Even if you're on fellowship, you have to really watch yourself, and books are expensive. I was trying to be good about my diet and not rely on the free pizza circuit where you go to all the lectures and conferences you can in order to get free food, but healthy food's expensive. I was scrounging for money, living on my own after my engagement went kaput. There was a time when I was sleeping on people's couches. I was in debt, trying to avoid taking out a student loan, but I ended up taking out loans through my credit card. That was definitely one source of stress, among many, that came through graduate school. I knew that the academic path would probably lead to a job at some point, but when was that going to happen? I wanted to get to work, and I wanted to be working with people. I was so tired of looking at libraries and reading, and this is coming from someone who is a literature major, you know? I just didn't want to look at books anymore. I started working as a personal trainer around that time because it coincided with my interests, and because it was very flexible, so I could actually schedule appointments around writing time, although eventually, I was scheduling writing time around my appointments. That met an immediate need, even though it wasn't going to be my career path. But it was a step in a direction that felt really positive; I was helping people be proactive about their health, to think seriously about nutrition.

Nursing was always the least likely thing I would go into. Part of my decision to go to nursing school was to conquer a part of myself that had always troubled me: on the one hand, I like to care for people and take care of people; but on the other hand, I have some gut reactions to certain things in hospitals that have made me fearful. Certain smells bother me, and I have this queasy feeling about blood and this and that. Until relatively recently, whenever I'd go into a hospital, I'd have instant anxiety. At the same time, my life has kind of led me in a direction where I've been taking care of people, starting with my grandparents, and then taking care of myself, and then taking care of personal training clients, who often do have lots of health issues that need to be accounted for and dealt with. I felt that maybe I should really think about nursing, even though it was, like, the exact opposite direction of where I would ever see myself going. But it can also be seen as remarkably linear from another perspective. It certainly helped that a lot of my family is in healthcare, and my mom is a retired RN, and my wife is a nurse.

Now that I'm about to finish nursing school, I realize that graduate school helped me prepare for this career. Nursing is a lot about teaching and research—otherwise you're doing the same things you were doing 20 years ago and wondering why people are getting infections in the hospital. It's interesting; people are saying the same things to me now that they were when I was an undergraduate. "You're time's up with this program, but you have these great research and writing skills. Maybe you should go on to an APRN program or consider a DNP program"—two degrees that merge nursing with graduate work, one of which is a doctorate. I'm seriously considering it. But I really would like to work for a while and see where that goes. I have the preparation for advanced work, I just have to decide whether or not I should be doing it. One of the biggest things I learned from grad school was that just because I can do something doesn't mean I should be doing it. Just because I have a good head on my shoulders, have a fairly good handle on language, and have the training for research and all that, that doesn't necessarily mean that's what I should be doing. But it might mean that I have a responsibility to help other people do it, though.

The nurse educator role is an exciting one. The best people who do that have at least one foot in the clinic, and can relate to the people in the rank and file rather than only to people who kind of go back and forth between the library and the research center. There's a place in nursing for pure research, but that's not where I want to be. Especially since I have aspirations of leadership in nursing and recruitment, I really feel as though I have a responsibility to have one foot in both arenas doing the research but also actually engaged in practice.

The idea of finishing my dissertation is still with me. I still talk about it in terms of unfinished business, but if I'm being really honest with myself, that's history, and what I'm doing now is where I'm going. I don't have any idea what it would take to get my mind back to that place. Moreover, I'm not really sure that I'd want to put myself through that again without a better handle on why I'm doing it, you know? At the time, getting it done and proving to myself that I could get it done was enough for a few years. But that's not a legitimate reason to me anymore. I don't have to finish just for the sake of finishing. I need a better reason than that. At this point in my life, I'm not going to take on anything unless it's going to have some profound meaning. I wouldn't take it back, going to grad school, but the best parts of it were the people I met, and the skills I learned—it made me smarter, gave me perspective, boosted my intellectual confidence, and taught me how to get work done.

It's funny though, topics come up all the time that make me think, once a graduate student, always a graduate student, because everything I see is a potential dissertation. It just keeps happening over and over again. I joke about it with some of the people in the program, like, oh, I bet no one's written about that yet, eh? And occasionally, I'll actually look in the archives to see if it's been done, and a lot of the time, it hasn't. One of the things that really interested me in grad school was racial formation theory, and that's not really a part of nursing practice. It's not part of the discourse, and that's a whole thing that's kind of open.

I have less than two months left, and then I take my boards. It was a two-year program condensed into one, without subtracting any of the hours, so it was kind of crazy, and I'm thankful that grad school prepared me for the level of reading. The only thing I detest are the exams, which are nothing like graduate school. I mean we didn't take exams in grad school, we wrote papers. So, funnily enough, when I get a chance to write a paper, it's like a gift because I can write papers. I just can't do these damn exams, you know?

In the coming year or so I'd like to still be living somewhere in the area, at the end of a good first year, and working a day shift—since I'll probably have to do the graveyard shift initially. And I'll be thinking about whether or not I'm giving this return-to-school thing a legitimate shot, you know? I do see teaching in the future. I'm not sure when, but I'd like to return to that. Not in the next year, but sometime in the future.

I'd also like to do some music on the side again. That's more challenging at my age because most people have a family by now, and other things going on. And, alas, especially in the rock scene, a lot of people have let themselves go. From a marketing standpoint, the band has to look good together and so I end up looking for people who are younger than me to work with because I haven't let myself go. I wouldn't want it to become a professional priority, since I really want to take my nursing career seriously, so maybe no going on tour. For now! Who knows what kind of nurse I'll be...I don't think I'll be typical, I can guarantee that much.

Chapter 8

Jason
Graduate Work in German Studies and Cinema Studies
Financial Services

The only thing I would say I regret—if anything—is that I wish I could have figured this out a few years faster. I kind of wish I could have come to this realization and made the big move maybe four years before I actually did.

Getting There

The expectations, when I was growing up, weren't necessarily to go to grad school—but to go to a good school, more generally. My parents were probably a bit troubled by the fact that I wasn't very serious about school during my first few years in college. I was really focused when it came to the stuff that I liked, but I totally blew off the stuff that I didn't like. In my sophomore year I decided I was going to be a history major—my parents' first question was like, "What are you going to do with that?" I initially thought, okay, yeah, law school, something like that.

But then I got serious about it in my junior year. I really got into the stuff I was studying, and started thinking about grad school and about going into academia. I think my parents were open to it. They probably assumed I would go on in something, since my sister went to law school, but they certainly didn't put pressure on me. But when I got my master's degree paid for, and then I got into PhD programs at really prestigious schools, they were like, "We don't care what you're doing, it's just great; keep it up!"

I only took a little time off after undergraduate. I was going to take two years off to work, and then go to grad school. But then the job I'd lined up started to fall through. And I was, quite frankly, really excited about stuff that I had been studying in my last two years. I didn't catch the academia bug until pretty late, and by then I was pretty fired up about it. I was getting into French theory and all sorts of interdisciplinary studies, doing a bit of architecture and film and literature and philosophy, and was sort of all over the place, and I just wanted to do more. So when the job wasn't happening, I was like, well, I don't know, maybe I don't need to take two years off. I talked to my intellectual history professor, because I thought that's sort of the direction I wanted to go, and he pointed me in the direction of the comparative literature department. They were like, "Oh yeah, you would fit in here perfectly." So I applied, got some money to cover tuition, and started after taking the summer and one semester off. I guess I did that for a year and a half, earning a master's degree.

I applied for PhD programs and for some grants at the same time. Got into a few schools, thought I was going to go. I was pretty much set to go to my top choice school on the East Coast; they're a big theory school, and I fancied myself a big theory-head. But I got this grant to go to Berlin and really dig into pre-1920s silent film and philosophy and Walter Benjamin and Frankfurt School stuff. So I took the grant instead, and while I was in Berlin decided that I was maybe less of a theory-head than I had thought, and really wanted to go in a bit of a different direction. So I came back after that fellowship year and went to Chicago, partly because my ex was there and we wanted to give things another try. I took some grad-level classes at a local university, filled out applications again, waited tables. I never expected to stay in Chicago. I was still thinking of some other schools on the East Coast, but they were really on the theory side, and I was thinking I wanted to be less theory-driven. In the end, the relationship didn't end up working out, but by then I'd already been swayed by people I'd met in the academic community, and I ended up staying in Chicago for the next nine years, on and off.

Getting Through

I really liked my program; and I mean, I still do. I think going there was by far the best decision I made. It's one of those places that's programmatically interdisciplinary. They really make a home for people to study whatever they find interesting, and to pursue that on their own. I ended up going into the German Studies department there, and then working on a joint degree with Cinema Studies. To do that at one of the other schools I considered, for example, I would have needed prerequisites in medieval German, in eighteenth-century German, in nineteenth-century German, and then in twentieth-century German. Even if I was just going to be a twentieth-century German guy, I would have had to go do all of these prerequisites. I was like, I don't really like German that much, I just want to do the film stuff. So my program was great—I can't say enough about the place. But the other side of that flexibility is that for someone like me who has really disparate interests and is extremely curious, and not incredibly disciplined about sitting down and writing every day, that might not be the best place. Unless you've got an advisor or a program that keeps you on a short enough leash.

I think I had a fairly good transition—with the exception of a pretty big issue at the end of my first year around incompletes. I'd gotten into my program and three or four other schools without actually having sent them my final transcripts from my master's school. I found out later from my advisor that they'd loved my writing sample, and thought I had really great recommendations, but they didn't really look at my grades so they didn't notice that I had five incompletes from my master's degree program. So, officially, I didn't have a master's degree at the end of my first year. At the start of the second year I was supposed to start teaching for my fellowship, but I couldn't be approved for teaching because it required a master's degree. So my advisor called me. She was like, "You're going to have to take next year off and finish all this stuff, and you need to have it done, and your master's degree in hand, by next year, today's date."

My issue has always been perfectionism—that was the reason for the incompletes—though I've been around the block enough to know that perfectionism is closely tied to insecurity. You want to do the most perfect thing, but you're also afraid of putting something out there that isn't extremely polished. I always did very well with professors who cut me no slack, like the grad advisor who said you need to finish all this shit; it better be in my office or I'm going to fail you. She got everything on time from me. What often happened is I'd do all this work, going at the glacial pace I imagined I needed to go to scour the earth for every bit of information that could be relevant to the brilliant idea that I had. But when it got down to it, it'd be like, okay, it's crunch time, and I've got to really get this thing done. It would still be really drafty. But it would be done, and usually what I found was that those were really good papers, and my professors really liked them, and that's what they wanted. I could see that pattern, but I wasn't able to turn it into a regular working style. I still haven't been able to turn that into a regular habit; I still have a hard time getting myself to churn things out.

So I took the year off, but I still had to earn a living so I got a job teaching reading enrichment classes to everyone from kids to adults. It was fairly exhausting. You do a lot of high-energy stuff, especially with the little kids where you have to do a lot of jumping up and down. I was working like five, six hours a day, and I only had six or seven hours a day when I could write. So I was incredibly productive for those seven hours. I ended up finishing one really big paper by Christmas, and that satisfied two of the incompletes. But I still had nine left, so I had to write nine papers in one quarter. I had 12 weeks to write nine papers. Incredibly stressful! But I learned how I work best.

I think one of the hardest things about graduate school is the lack of regular feedback, and recognition for all the stuff you're doing. At first, you turn in papers at the end of the quarter. But once you get into the upper levels of your program, you aren't turning in papers every quarter; you're getting much less feedback, and when you do get it, it's weightier—it matters more. Psychologically, it's like you don't get meals on a regular enough basis to keep you going. With my job now, I get to complete things multiple times a week, and I get that satisfaction of like, done, done; off the table. That has helped me adjust to the idea of doing things much more quickly. I mean, my first boss here used to always say to me just write—whatever—write the report, write the e-mail. Don't do it perfectly, just get it done.

I remember once, back in grad school, I hadn't seen my dissertation advisor for at least four or five months and I think I owed him a draft of something. I was speaking at a conference we had on campus, and I followed my normal M.O., which is to prepare, prepare, prepare, prepare. It took me six weeks to write the first page and a half, and then I stayed up all night the night before the conference and wrote the rest of it—another nine pages. I actually missed the first part of the conference; sort of ran in there after printing the thing out about 20 minutes before my panel started. So I get there, and I go up to present, and I see my advisor in the back row, up at the top of the amphitheater. I was convinced that he was thinking: what a fucking idiot; I can't believe that I've been backing this guy for so long. Then during the Q&A session I picked a fight with this other school of thought, which started a big debate—and my advisor backed me up. Then he came down afterward, and he was like, "Great to see you; I thought your paper was brilliant." It was really great, of course—it obviously still stands out in my memory—but as unbelievably fantastic as it felt, it was also really weird. There's something wrong with the fact that I had so much riding on my advisor's response, and that the profession doesn't let people feel better on a regular basis about the stuff that they're doing. I had this moment where I was able to step away and be like, yeah, this feels really great, but it's really wrong that this is how things work.

After my year off, finishing incompletes, I came back for another two years to do coursework and exams. Then after my exams, I went to Europe for a year with my girlfriend, which ended up not being productive for me at all. I was technically doing research. I just didn't get any done. All of the good things I learned about getting work done during the year of the incompletes, those lessons didn't stick at that point. At some level, I realized that to be really successful in academia,

I would need to have a schedule like I did that year. But those work habits were born out of necessity. You can't really fake necessity. I couldn't go to my advisors throughout my career and say, you're going to need to threaten to fire me once a year if I don't get my stuff done.

When I came back from Europe I got a really great two-year position helping students through a one-year master's program. The university wanted these students to be successful, so they hired a bunch of advanced graduate students to help them through. I had 12 students in my group, and I was their advisor, coach, and therapist, all at the same time. There's some classroom teaching, but you spend a lot of time extracting work from them. Like, "All right, I need to hear an idea for your thesis." Then later, "Okay now I need to see a one-page abstract of your thesis." Then, "I need to see the introduction, plus a bibliography." We'd extract work, then meet with them, and workshop their materials throughout the year, always pushing them to complete whatever they were working on. Again I was incredibly good at that; I was good at cracking the whip, good at helping others be really productive. But, yeah, it obviously didn't translate into me then turning around and cranking out my dissertation.

Moving On

It was at the end of that two-year position that I really started thinking there were probably other things I could do, other things I could be good at. I'd see an ad for a paralegal or something like that, and I'd think, shit, I can do all that stuff, and I'd be better than those people. I knew I could teach at any level. I talked about union organizing with a friend of mine. But there was never the confidence that I would be really good, or that I'd really enjoy doing something else. You don't really feel empowered to go and try other things because the costs are too great at that point—the stakes are too high. You've devoted a ton of time to school. And I liked it. I was really good at it, except for not being able to finish papers fast enough. I still thought this whole academia thing should somehow work out for me.

But some of it wasn't working, including the finances. I had a stipend for my first four years, and at the time it was the most amount of money they were giving out—$12,000 a year. Two years later, the people coming in got like $17,000 a year and another $3,000 thrown on top for the summer. There was no changing that. Some people were getting by on $12,000 a year and some were getting by on $20,000. Then, of course, the stipend ends after four years. I started taking out loans at some point and once I opened the door to that, it didn't stop; every year I took out another one. That was something that was really stupid, frankly. I didn't sit down and think, okay, this will at some point equal a payment of $625 dollars a month; I just thought, well, whatever. Down the road, I'll be employed, and blah, blah, blah. You know, you find yourself sitting around with a whole bunch of really, really, really smart people, and you're all making the same mistakes, trying to figure this out. Occasionally one of your friends has an idea about all this stuff, about how the interest rates are going to make it easier to deal with down the road, and you'd listen to that person like they were a genius, and who knows if they knew what they were talking about. I think the university tried to offer some guidance on those things, but there needs to be another reality check. Someone who says, look, if you end up in graduate school for an additional six years and you're taking out $18,000 a year, it's going to add up to this much money. That could be a down payment on an apartment that you're not going to be able to buy because you're paying off that loan. Yeah, it was difficult, it was hard to make ends meet.

I went to New York for the summer—I had access to my sister's apartment while she was away—and my plan was to buckle down and hammer out my dissertation proposal. I was going to find a job in a kitchen there, because that's something I'd done before, and I really liked food. But it didn't work out right away, and I was really broke. So I was scouring craigslist, and I wasn't a huge fan of George Bush, and I see this ad that says, "Hey, do you want to help defeat George Bush?" So I call the number, I go in for this interview, and it's for a fundraising job—like standing on the streets of New York stopping people and asking them for money which I thought was completely crazy—the last place on the planet you want to stop people. As it turned out, it was a great deal of fun, and I was really, really good at it—I ended up being the top fundraiser across the country. I would stop anybody and would get them to part with cash. Sometimes large amounts of cash! That was my first big break with academia. I did that all summer, and did not end up writing my dissertation proposal.

At the end of the summer I was offered a position to work on getting out the vote in battleground states, and I was like, "Look, I can't. I really have to go now and write my dissertation." So of course I drove back to Chicago through all these battleground states, thinking about the offer, and by the time I arrived, I called them back and was like, "All right, I am doing this." So I went to Ohio, and I had a team of 25 people, and then underneath them there were another 100 people. It was a really amazing experience, also extremely emotional, and at the end of it, this couple who'd become my adopted family asked me what I did in real life. I told them I was in graduate school, that I was going back. They were surprised. They were like, "We thought you'd be an organizer or something; you're really great at this." It was one of those pivotal conversations. I really needed someone to say just that. Then I was able to say the same thing: I guess I am really good at this.

When I got back to Chicago after that, I worked part time for a fund-raising company, cranked out my dissertation proposal and defended it in the spring. Then my old boss from the earlier fund-raising job offered me a job back in New York that would have paid me what was, at the time, comparable to what I would have made as an assistant professor. I think it was like $55,000. I was like, well, shit. I can move to New York City and get paid as much as I would get paid to be an assistant professor, and I can do it today. So, yeah, a couple weeks later, I moved to New York. I told my friends I was moving, of course, but I didn't tell my advisors since it was summer and everyone was gone anyway, and at that point I didn't know how long I'd be away.

I wasn't sure it was going to take. I kept my apartment in Chicago; I sublet it, but kept all my stuff there, and all my books, and didn't un-enroll from school. I was nervous that I wouldn't be able to get up and go to work every day. I just thought, I've had it too easy for too many years. I don't know if I can do proper hard work. I can do it for a summer, but that's not like a position where you've only got two weeks of vacation. So I was a bit nervous. But yeah, I did it, and I loved it. I thrived on it. It was sort of like that year I had to take off to finish the incompletes; I had to go in every day, and there were people who relied on me, and I had targets to hit. There was definitely a lot of pressure, but it's a different type of pressure than the more psychological kind you get in academia. I think I deal with it better. I perform really well under that different, nonacademic type of pressure.

I left officially a year later. I haven't thought about it much, and haven't talked about it much, but I think the hardest part was leaving the people and the milieu. I mean, it was happening anyway—people from my year were leaving to do research for their dissertations, and in a few more years they'd be leaving to take postdocs, or jobs. I would have lost touch with people anyway. But leaving over the summer when I moved to New York was odd, because a lot of people were just gone for the season—and then I was gone too, but unlike everyone else, I wasn't coming back. There was no chance to say goodbye to the people I knew primarily from campus. I just disappeared.

The biggest challenge with telling my family was my mom, who was always asking me, "Are you going to finish?" She kept asking for years; I think she's tapered off now because I've made it clear: why would I ever do that? Why would I take the time, now, to write a dissertation? It just makes no sense. But she was still psychologically invested for a long time. My dad was like, "Hey, go work. That's great. You're loving it and you're good at it, so get out there and make some money, damn it." I think some people were sort of shocked, but I think most people were like, "Yeah, that makes a certain degree of sense; you're interested in a lot of different things, and you don't really listen to people anyway." There was a certain amount of risk involved, but I think the short-term jobs in Ohio and then in New York gave me a better, more realistic sense of my chances of succeeding outside of academia. One of the best things about those experiences was that they helped me see that leaving was risky, but not crazy—I knew I could do it.

I was in New York for a bit over two years, hiring and training and managing teams of fundraisers around the city, and going door to door to raise money for children's charities. At the end of that, I was like, even though I'm getting paid better than I used to get paid, I'm working way too hard for the amount of money I'm making. I got in touch with the friend of a grad school friend who was hiring for a major company that works with financial market data. The grad school friend and I had talked a lot about whether or not to leave academia—and he left too—so he knew that I was open to doing different things. He talked to his friend who was hiring and he was like, "Yeah, this guy can *sell* shit. He does charity stuff, but he can really sell." Because that's essentially what I was doing—fundraising is essentially just selling. You're just selling something different. Yeah, there was a certain amount of risk involved as well, because it was a whole different world. I didn't know anything about finance. I didn't know the difference between a stock and a bond, and really had no clue. But I was ready to take the risk, and I went in there and had a really great interview. Now I work for a big corporation with over 50,000 people—and in a totally different field; I'm deeply involved with financial services. I started out selling market data to banks. So it was definitely a really big, different world.

My first two years were really, really difficult. I was working in the Frankfurt office and I wasn't terribly happy about going back to Germany, partly just because I was bored with the place. I had been going back and forth and studying German stuff for like 20 years, so I was not too pleased about it, but I was like, I can do this, because this is going to give me the chance to start a new, exciting career, and if I do well, I can move to wherever the hell I want. But it was difficult. I'm not sure if it was difficult because it was corporate, or because it was German, or some mixture of both. In any case, I didn't do very well—the learning phase was rough, and what they'd given me to do wasn't fun. But by the second year I was doing really well, even though I still wasn't super happy there. All my close friends were journalists, and I made sort of a strong push to move into that industry. So I wasn't yet convinced I was on the right path. I had a really hard time imagining myself in finance five years down the road. But by the end of the second year things sort of clicked. I was performing really well, and starting to be recognized by my peers as an expert in certain areas. It was kind of like the transition in grad school from being a beginning student, to being well on the other side of your master's degree and your qualifying exams—when you're a "senior grad student" or whatever, and you're comfortable sitting in the room with whichever professor is there and just talking about the things you know. Figuring it out, and being compensated really well was great, but it wasn't enough for me to be able to imagine a future there. What was missing was recognition. So when I started to get that, when people were coming to me for my help, and my opinions, then it all turned around. Then a job in London came up, and I moved here, and that really did it—that completed my ability to imagine sticking around and having a future. I'm at a point now where there are options—and they're right ahead of me. I can see sticking around. I can see leaving, to be honest. But I'm more comfortable in this strange corporate environment than I ever thought I would be or could be.

I still have a recurring date in my calendar; the day I paid off my credit card debt. It was the first time since I was 18 years old that I had been free of that debt. It took me 20 years to pay it off, and I was like, this feels fucking great. Now—I mean, I got married last year, and now I'm about to have a kid, and I can't imagine. It would have scared the crap out of me to do either of those things ten years ago. In retrospect, I think that my financial instability might have made it easier for me to stay away from completely committing myself to someone. I think that sort of financial insecurity has really deep tentacles that I've only discovered in reverse. Now, I can say to myself, all right, I'm not going to starve, and the people who are with me aren't going to starve. There's a lot of psychological comfort there, and it's pretty strong.

The only thing I would say I regret—if anything—is that I wish I could have figured this out a few years faster. I kind of wish I could have come to this realization and made the big move maybe four years before I actually did. But then, again, the hard thing about regretting the timing is that I don't think I'd be as good at what I do now, if I hadn't taken the route that I did then. There's a lot from my graduate student years that set me up really well to do both the fundraising job and my current job. And there's a lot about the fundraising job in particular that's probably essential to where I am today. Yeah, you can't plan for that.

Chapter 9

Tony
Graduate Work in Literature
Academic Dean

I think this career is a great fit for me—though I didn't even know it existed when I was training for it, so there was no way for me to have had it on my radar as a goal. Actually, it's just the opposite—it's precisely what was missing for me in graduate school, that I ended up turning into an area of expertise.

Getting There

I went to grad school for so many different reasons. Throughout school, I enjoyed literature more than any other subject, and talking about it, critiquing it, and interpreting it were always really interesting to me. My lit classes as an undergrad were great; I loved most of them, and was still excited about the ones that I didn't like, because I thought I could probably improve upon them. So, I always felt a pull in that direction—I wanted to be a professor. Also, I went to three different colleges during my undergrad career, so I didn't feel like I'd had the experience that other people had and I wanted it. I'd always wanted to travel internationally—maybe spend some time going to school in Europe or Ireland—and I thought grad school might be a way to do that. I suppose I just wasn't ready to be done with school yet, to be frank. But I also got a lot of encouragement from my professors and it seemed like a good way to pursue a couple of different intersecting interests, and still make progress toward a career.

It was an amorphous sort of goal that didn't really take shape for a long time. There's this sense that for a liberal arts student to get a graduate degree and then teach—well, there's so many that go down that path. The way has been paved by millions of people so it's a pretty obvious path, and one that doesn't require a lot of guidance... So I didn't get much guidance, even though I really could have used it. I didn't know what steps to take, or what to do. Basically my plan for getting into grad school was to make sure I met all the requirements to graduate, and try to get really good grades. I went to the library and figured out what tests I had to take and what the process was, when the deadlines were. I did speak to an advisor who was overwhelmed by the number of students she was supposed to advise, so it wasn't all that helpful. I made my way through the process eventually, and it worked. Though I'm not sure I would have gone to the same school for my master's—which was the same school where I did my undergrad—if I'd had more guidance.

I thought about trying to get into a school in Europe, but the system is different, and really complicated. At some point it was just easier to stay where I was, where I knew my way around. I had friends who were in grad school, and I went to a state school that had a graduate program in my field, so the local setting had some aspects that were really clear and legible in a situation that was, otherwise, pretty unclear and confusing. I was in love with academia, you know? Ivy covered walls, wandering around with a bag of books, everybody waving at each other. It was all there at my school, so why look further? I didn't know it at the time, and it's one of those things that no one really talks about until further along in the process, but the ivy quickly loses out to internal politics, and an incredibly difficult job market. There's tenure-track versus nontenured jobs, and people end up cobbling together a living through teaching positions at three or four different junior colleges. But I didn't know any of that stuff. If I had, I think I would have pursued grad school in a different fashion. I might have gone somewhere with fewer students who were better positioned to be competitive later.

Getting Through

It was a pretty seamless transition. I finished school, took a little time off, then went right back to the same classrooms, had some of the same teachers. Some of my friends were lecturers in the program. It was just as fun as it was the year before, but it wasn't as challenging. It wasn't until we got into the more interpretive analysis that it became challenging and fun again. Those were the classes that made me think, someday I would love to teach a class like this.

Later I found out that in order to teach a class like that, you had to do a zillion things first—one of which was to fulfill a kind of apprenticeship by being a lecturer. When my turn came, I lectured for a survey of British literature filled with fraternity dudes. They made up about 60 percent of the class and had zero interest in the material. Thirty percent were marginally interested in literature, and ten percent were really committed because they wanted a good grade. It was a constant struggle, trying to get people interested. That's when I started thinking I might not want to be a professor. You'd have to teach a billion of those classes before you could even consider proposing a new course to the administration, then it would have to go through a bunch of channels, and then it gets watered down and altered to ensure that it is lock step with the rest of the curriculum and that it doesn't launch anybody too far beyond the survey course that they're taking simultaneously. All of those things, by the way, are meritable, laudable goals. You need those processes in order to have a cohesive curriculum. But it sounds like a drag, you know, when you're just taking a class and you think, oh, this is a cool class; I would love to teach this class and then, you know, take sabbatical.

Meanwhile, for the most part, they're not on sabbatical. Or they're on sabbatical working their tails off, or using summers to write and publish in order to remain relevant and retain the classes that they want to teach or have created. There's this misconception about academia, this error in perception that lasts until you finish undergrad and decide to stay in the system. It seems totally doable, like you could get involved in this chain of events at the beginning, and come out at a predictable, desirable place at the end. And, if everything goes just right, it could be that way. Some of my friends were truly brilliant, they had interpretive minds and that launched them into superstardom in academia, you know, so they got the gig that they wanted pretty quickly and every step that they took seemed like the next logical step in the process; you buy a house off campus and have summers off and a sabbatical, and wonderful classes that you love to teach, and then you eventually becoming chair and that kind of thing. All of it sounds so cool when you're looking at it from the outside. But you could be in for a rude awakening. Or a bright morning, but mostly it's a rude awakening.

I finished my master's degree after a little more than two years, and even though I was a bit disillusioned after my teaching experiences, I still wanted to continue. What else are you going to do? A master's degree in literature is a little bit more useful than a bachelor's degree when it comes to defining a career but I wanted more options. I didn't feel like I had a better plan, so whether it was tarnished or not, I was going to pursue the one that I did have. I had done well in my degree program, and I had great letters of recommendation. I applied to six or eight schools and I was accepted to one that I was particularly interested in because they were open to the idea of me doing an interdisciplinary PhD. Again, I did things in what I thought was the most logical order possible—I took courses in the required sequence and I did all the teaching that I could but the plan for the rest of my PhD was hazy, even after I'd been there for a considerable amount of time. My advisors seemed to like the idea of having an amorphous PhD program, and there was a sense that they were going to guide a handful of students through it, and at the end we would all be really well-educated beneficiaries of their insight and wisdom. Sadly, they were working all the time; when did they have time to create and divulge wisdom, you know?

When it came time to teach, again, I struggled with trying to lecture effectively to people who were just summarily, and actively, disinterested in the material. For a while I took it as kind of a challenge, thinking that someone who was meant to be a teacher could, you know, *Dead Poet's Society* them and really get them turned around and engaged. But over time it made me stop loving literature, because when I would read anything I'd start imagining how I'd try to convince an imaginary student that it was important, that it was relevant. Looking back, I think the lack of pedagogical training was a real problem; learning sound and simple pedagogical processes—how to create a class, how to make the material challenging, and how to respond when students challenged the material—that would have made a significant difference. At the time, though, I just felt guilty about working with students who really needed guidance that I wasn't able to provide, and working with class structures that made it difficult to deliver good information.

And that lack of pedagogical structure, unfortunately, pervaded the program—showing up in the classes I was taking, and in the way the program was structured. There was, for example, a surprising amount of leeway around which courses I could take, and what kinds of activities I could apply toward my PhD. That's lovely on paper, however, as a result, I never had to sit down and say, I want to focus on this one specific problem. I think the idea was to let the process unfold more organically, for me to follow my interests and see where I ended up—and then at that point, I would receive more specific guidance from my advisors about what courses to take next, and in what order, and how they would apply to my program moving forward. But there was a lot of confusion, and since I didn't have much guidance or a specific objective, I didn't know where to locate the confusion—whether it was internal to me, or external and part of the program. Everyone else seemed like they knew what they were talking about—they were all so blasé and I had no idea. I think of it as the "hide and seek PhD." Stuff I needed was really well known by people three or four years ahead of me, but they were unavailable. I have acquaintances who went through the same program and they flourished and did great. When you have a precise goal you can chart a path through an unstructured space. But if your goal itself is unstructured then you need a really structured space to help you get where you need to be. It was a great idea for how to run a PhD program, but it wasn't a good fit for me. It would have been so helpful if a more advanced grad student, or a new professor, would have said, yeah, I went through all of that stuff. It's a morass—impossible to understand. Don't try to get a meta-perspective on it now, not while you're stuck in the middle. Just chart your way through; set your own goals and once you're done, then you can look back and interpret the whole experience. Unfortunately, that never happened.

The program's flexibility did help me in some major ways, even if it was hindering me in others. I had a job on campus and I worked all the time but I wasn't able to earn enough; I mean, I was barely getting by. So I asked if I could try to find a teaching gig somewhere else as long as I maintained regular correspondence with my panel and mentors—and, would they allow teaching at another university to count toward the teaching requirements for the PhD? They agreed, and so that's what I did. I got a great job in Prague, in the Czech Republic, in American studies. The students were nonnative English speakers but they were at such a level that it was not an issue. Suddenly, it felt great to be teaching. I was a professor there, not a graduate student, and I was teaching classes that I understood, and it seemed like the students came from a tradition of accepting education. I didn't have to try to talk them into being engaged and interested; they already were. They went to class, and did their homework, and took it all seriously.

It was what I thought being a professor would be like. I would get up and take the train to school and drink coffee and eat breakfast in a really lovely lounge, then go to my office and read students' papers and prepare for class. Then I'd go to class, lecture, return papers, have discussion, repeat that a couple of times throughout the day, and then go home. I'd go out with colleagues afterward, or with friends, and have a few beers and some pizza and then go home and do it again. There was lots of time scheduled within the work day to do the tasks that are necessary to be an academic professor. There were hours where I got paid to sit in a room and write, read papers and respond, or prepare lessons. Even when my teaching schedule came back around to the same class again, you know, six months later or a year later, I was still given the same amount of time to prepare—which doesn't always happen in American academia. You don't always get a bunch of time to review the content of your course, you should know it already, right? It was lovely. When I finished work, when I finished at school, that was the end of the work day and I didn't have any other obligations—my evenings and weekends were my own.

Summers were also really great because I worked at a language institute, which is what a lot of the faculty members who weren't from the Czech Republic did, especially those who spoke English. I had the same hours, nine to three, and I taught a couple of classes, but mostly I developed a language school curriculum starting from zero fluency to completely fluent and I got to look at the whole spectrum and start breaking it up and seeing what the signposts mean, how people progress through it, and what the best teaching practices are. This is when I started really considering what pedagogy means and how it works. By the end, I had developed a complete curricular program and system with exams and texts and all kinds of stuff, so it was fun, really invigorating.

That was a great environment; it was a beautiful place. I felt like I had made a demonstrable step in my professional life and I wasn't just in school anymore like I had been forever. Then I was asked to take on a role that was similar to what we'd consider the chair of the program and I thought, gosh it's probably because I'm doing such a good job! Honestly it was probably because I was American, and it was an American studies program. But I think I must have been doing an okay job because in the new role I got to design the program and work with the teachers and look at the curriculum and how it was linked together. It had been developed in a very specific historical style that didn't really indicate what goes on in America, so we got to redo it, which was exciting. Between the summer language institute curriculum development, and redesigning the American studies program, I started to really get a taste for what would become my future career—academic administration—a different part of academia that doesn't require 20 years of struggling.

I was supposed to be gone for six to nine months and I just loved it; I didn't want to come back so I wrote and said, I'll be back later. They said, okay, and I stayed there for four years. I could have stayed even longer, but I was increasingly bothered by the sense that I hadn't completed my PhD. In addition, there were some difficulties associated with living in the Czech Republic; there were a lot of tensions around immigrant populations and I felt a surprising level of close-mindedness among my colleagues. Also, it's difficult to get a retirement program going there or start a 401(k), which makes planning for the future more difficult. And maybe, over time, it didn't feel like it was challenging enough anymore. So that was that.

Moving On

I came back home, but I came to Southern California rather than going back to my grad school program. My relationship with my mom, who lived in the region, had been somewhat troubled, and I wanted to try to sort that out. Also, I just wanted to be here and be around in case she needed something because many of my siblings had moved away from Los Angeles. In addition, I was in a relationship with someone that lived in the same area. We'd started dating while I was in Prague, and when things got more serious, it became another reason to come back. I'd loved being in the northwest before, but between the constant rain, memories of the deep confusion that had plagued me there, and family commitments in SoCal, coming to LA seemed like a no-brainer.

I still wanted to finish, and my family was like, "Hey, are you going to do that, dude? We wanted to call you doctor!" So I did some preliminary investigation into whether I might be able to transfer from my former program to a school in LA. But it's complicated, as you can imagine. At first it was on my mind a lot, but I had so much else going on as well. I was in a relationship, figuring out a new city, I was making a bunch of friends—so a year went by when I didn't think about it at all. Then, to be honest, it was hard to fathom how it would even be possible. I didn't want to move back to my grad program, but it didn't seem like I'd be able to finish from LA. If I did move back, I'd have to give up my job, and then how would I pay for everything? I hadn't been in school for four years, and I was really happy living a post-student lifestyle. I enjoyed being able to make a car payment and pay rent on a real apartment, and have a relationship with someone, and buy Christmas gifts and all that stuff. Going back to school felt like it would require a certain amount of lifestyle regression.

At the same time, it was becoming more clear to me that I liked the administrative and structural side of academia more than the research and teaching side—what I've considered the more cutthroat "do or die" side. You know, it's funny, but after living in Prague and focusing on pedagogy and academic structure in several professional contexts, that's how I figured out that's what was missing from my grad school experience. And that led to me thinking that's what I should try to provide. This might sound high-minded, but I felt like the traditional tenure-track path would set people up to teach classes filled with individuals, whereas going into administration with a focus on pedagogy would allow me to teach faculty how to teach which would reach far more people and make a much bigger difference. Also, it was more interesting for me to talk about the most effective ways of delivering information and helping students learn, than to talk about poetry with students.

So I worked at a language school that was affiliated with a state university, and then I became director of the school—and that's probably when I realized, finally, that I wasn't going to finish the PhD. Then I worked as the director of another university-affiliated school where all of the students came from other countries and they were fluent in English but not 100 percent fluent. Lots of schools in Europe and Asia graduate students a bit earlier than we do here, so there's a window of time when it's really perfect for them to come to the United States and perfect their English, and take college-level courses at the same time. As director, it was really interesting for me to work on language curricula with the goal of delivering students to college-level courses, including, ironically, surveys of British and American Literature. As a result of feeling lost for a while in my own education, it made a lot of sense for me to try to help the professors who were teaching these kids—help them understand course structures, lesson plans, and stuff like that.

So I did that, and I loved it, and then I was invited to apply for a deanship at a music and arts school—and that's where I am now. It's a pretty traditional academic role that ensures that all of the school's courses and programs adhere to the internal mandates and structures of the school as well as to the external mandates and structures of various governing bodies—all while trying to find ways for us to do an even better job meeting our responsibilities and serving students. It's interesting that my education started out highly structured, and then became much less so in my PhD program, and then started coming back around when I went to Europe and worked in

different cultures with lots of different professors who taught
me a lot about how students learn. Now I'm back here applying what I've learned in higher education. That's the arc of my
education! To be honest, finishing the PhD now would be of
very little service to me; it would just be for my ego, I suppose.
I feel like I've already completed my education. There's enough
tweed and ivy in my career for me to feel like I'm living the
academic fantasy I always wanted.

I find that the majority of the students at my school are
probably in the position I was in when I finished my bachelor's
degree. They're younger, but they don't know what the hell
they're going to do and they don't really have a lot of tools
to figure out how to do it. They're all artists which is doubly
challenging because they don't care for rules, you know? So I
feel like, in my position now, I really do have the opportunity
to serve those students who are very much like I was at one
point. It feels much more rewarding to me to deliver clarity,
structure, and strategy to students than to deliver a survey of
American Literature before World War II. Another great thing
is that all the students at the school where I work now—they're
all motivated and following their dream. 100 percent want to
be there—as opposed to the earlier teaching experience I mentioned, where maybe ten percent wanted to be there. It's really
rewarding to work around a bunch of people who are pursuing their dream; however, it's also very challenging because lots
of them are not going to succeed, you know, in what they're
studying. However, they could always become an academic
administrator; apparently that's an option!

But seriously, I think this career is a great fit for me—though
I didn't even know it existed when I was training for it, so
there was no way for me to have had it on my radar as a goal.
Actually, it's just the opposite—it's precisely what was missing
for me in graduate school, that I ended up turning into an

area of expertise. I always wanted to work in academia; it's an endeavor—the endeavor—that seems the most urgent, and the most important to me so it's great to have found a career that matches my interests and skills with a structural need. In the next couple of years I plan to finish a secondary master's degree in academic administration and leadership, with a focus on multi-scale curricula: planning, structure and pedagogy. Having that will allow me and my wife the freedom to move most anywhere. It would be nice, as a next step, to move into a deanship focused on compliance or curricula development at a not for profit liberal arts college somewhere—West Coast would be nice, but Chicago is a great city too, except that it freezes all the time but you know, I wouldn't say no to the right job. Europe still calls occasionally and we talk sometimes about living there—maybe later. Eventually, I'd like to stop working and write some of what I've learned in the form of a meta-structured curriculum on how to create curricula—a step-by-step process, the arc of curricular development, and within that, how users—university leaders—would develop individual tools for their program. Nerdy, I know, but really exciting too. Maybe I could write that from Europe...

Interview: Lauren Willig
Graduate Work in History; Law Degree
Novelist, *The Pink Carnation* series (ten and counting), *2L*, and *The Ashford Affair*, among others

You are so prolific, it's hard to believe you haven't been a novelist for your entire adult life. And yet, there was a "before," wasn't there?

I had been in training to be a writer since I was very small. I knew from an early age that I wanted to be a novelist, preferably a historical novelist. I'd grown up reading Writer's Digest and all the other trade journals, I'd interned at a publishing house while I was in college, and I had a very realistic view of how hard it was to make a life as an author. I had always assumed that if I was going to be a novelist, it would be part of a two-career life—that I would have a sustainable career, and then write in my spare time. Writing—just writing—seemed like a nineteenth-century bohemian fantasy that involved starving in a garret. So, coming out of undergrad, my plan was to go to graduate school—English History at Harvard—where I'd learn more about the historical eras that interested me the most, and lay the groundwork for a career as an academic. I had a charmingly naïve view of a career where I would teach during the school year and write historical fiction during summers. This, obviously, was before I realized exactly how overworked junior faculty actually are.

Was it what you expected?

I adored my first two years. I couldn't imagine anything more attractive than being immersed in my favorite time periods. The main surprise for me was the historiographical emphasis. As it turned out, getting a history PhD is not the preparation for novel writing that I'd imagined it to be. I was used to old-fashioned political history, and to being very hands-on with the primary sources—focusing on a kind of history that's about what happened when. It was a little jarring to shift to a historiographical approach, which is more about how historians have viewed history over time, and less about the actual day-to-day of history. The larger questions and issues that you deal with in grad school are not the kinds of details you need to write fiction. It's history at a meta-level, which isn't necessarily useful for trying to recreate a historical world from the ground up.

What about the later years, the qualifying exams, and dissertation prospectus?

I was one of those weirdoes who enjoyed qualifying exams. Of course, we heard all sorts of stories about the hideous things that happened during the exam, but I have a background in debate and public speaking and so I thought they were kind of fun. It was a different story, though, when it came time for the dissertation prospectus. In honor of me passing my generals and two of his other students getting jobs, my advisor hosted a dinner party which included a couple of other distinguished historians. I mentioned my dissertation topic and one of them turned to me and said "Oh didn't you're hear? So-and-so has just finished a manuscript on that very issue." I had to scramble to come up with something else, and while I did come up with something that intrigued me, it turned out that it was one of those topics that hadn't been done before for a reason—in this case, because it was really difficult to find the source material. (For those who might be curious, the topic was Royalist Conspiracies during the Latter Half of the English Civil Wars, 1646–1649. As I learned the hard way, conspirators seldom leave written records. In fact, it's far safer for them not to.) In retrospect, knowing what I know now, it was the sort of topic that would have made a great second book but was a horrible dissertation topic because it required a high level of familiarity with extraneous sources that were really hard to track down. You just don't have that acquired wisdom as a novice researcher, coming straight out of your general exams.

Nevertheless, I got a grant and went off to England to do my dissertation research. It was while I was in England that I made the decision to leave grad school. There were a number of different factors that ultimately played into the decision. I didn't know any other grad students there, so it was lonely, and a very abrupt departure from the camaraderie of the history department. It was an ongoing struggle to find the sorts of sources I needed, which made the research incredibly frustrating. And I realized that I hadn't loved teaching. So put those two together, and it was kind of like, okay, if I'm not doing this for the research, or for the teaching, what's holding me to this career?

This sounds like a big moment for you. Were you certain at that point that you were going to leave?

No, I actually decided to leave it up to fate. I decided to submit one application to law school—to Harvard Law, because it was right down the block from the history department and, if I got in, I could finish my PhD while I was going to law school. At that point I had completed four years already. The average for the history PhD was seven—if you were relatively speedy. I figured, with four years down, I could do law school and finish the last three of my PhD at the same time. And, if I didn't get into that one law school, I would go back to the dissertation, and see about making a career for myself as an academic. In March I found out that I had gotten in, so off I went to law school, leaving myself the option of deciding, at the end of it, whether I wanted to give academia another chance or if I wanted to just say the hell with it and work at a law firm for a while. After having gone straight from undergrad to grad school, there was also something very appealing about the idea of living in the real world for a little bit and having that kind of office-based professional experience. The grass is always greener!

It sounds feasible, laid out like that. But you started your writing career in the midst of this, right?

I did, though I didn't realize at the time that I was launching a third career! Right after my general exams I had begun working on a novel just for fun. I'd realized that the kind of history I was doing was not necessarily conducive to novel writing. To avoid becoming stilted, to remember the fun of history, I needed to start working on a novel sooner rather than later. So as soon as my general exams were done and my advisor told me to take the summer off before turning to my dissertation, I started writing a novel. I finished it while I was in England and sent it to an agent, then got a call that summer with the news that he wanted to represent me. Everything moved very, very quickly after that. The call came in August, and I wound up with a two-book contract by October—just as I was starting law school. It wasn't my first novel; I'd written, and submitted, and had novels rejected in the past. I was surprised that the one

I wrote after my exams was the one that hit, because that was the one I had written just for fun. The best things tend to happen by accident when you're not expecting them.

When I got the contract I was absolutely delighted—it was something I'd wanted, and worked toward, my entire life. But it wasn't yet, in my mind, a career. I still had strong associations between writing for a living and starving in a garret. But it was highly gratifying to have success in the field that meant the most to me.

So, you're starting law school which is already intense— but with the addition of both a dissertation and a book contract. How did you keep it all straight?

The contract was what really threw a wrench into my original law school/dissertation plan. All of a sudden I had revisions to do on the first book manuscript, and a contract for a second manuscript which was due a year later, and a full first-year course load at school. All of my spare time went to the novel; I didn't have any left for the dissertation. The following year it got harder: I signed a contract for two more books, and I wound up taking a summer job at a law firm, which meant I didn't have the summer off to write a book. Things were pretty insane by my third year of law school: the work was more intense, the stakes were higher, and the production schedules for my novels were getting shorter.

Fortunately, law school is a bit like college in that once you figure out the rhythms, it's easy to adjust your class schedule to make it fit around the rest of your life. I still, at that point, thought I was going to finish the blasted dissertation. I was also able to be a bit more relaxed about law school itself because the world was different then. The legal industry was going through a boom time; law students knew that employers needed them. Even the kids who were in the middle of the class were going to land at good firms. I took classes that interested me rather than the ones I thought would impress lawyers, so of course I did better in them, because I found them entertaining. (Who doesn't love Ancient Athenian Legal History?) On top of that, it helped that I grew up in a legal family and had internalized a certain amount of legal thinking over the dinner table. I wouldn't be able to take the same laid-back approach now. I have two siblings who have gone to law school postrecession, and the attitude is really very different all around. Now, everyone knows that the market is tough, and jobs are scarce, so people take their work very, very seriously.

How many novels did you write during law school?

I wound up writing three books when I was in law school, with successively tighter deadlines. The third came out about two months after I graduated, took the bar, and started working at a firm—and I had one more under contract that I needed to finish.

So three books in, you were still thinking that you needed a backup career. Was it definitely going to be law at this point, or did academia still have a place in your heart?

I went into law firm life still thinking that I'd finish the dissertation, but it was becoming increasingly abstract to me. I knew at that point I was not going back into academia as a career; even if I finished the dissertation, the odds of getting a job were slim. At the same time, though, I wasn't completely committed to a career in law. It was a wildcard to me—I was open to enjoying it, but I wasn't sure that I would. I figured I would see how I reacted to it, see whether or not I loved practicing law, and plan my life accordingly—but without giving up the writing. The writing was always the first priority.

Were you able to do both—juggle your first year at a law firm, and your writing commitments?

I was, for a short period of time. Even if circumstances hadn't permitted me to leave after a year and a half, it wouldn't have been sustainable in the long term. When I started writing, the author's job was to produce a manuscript, and then the publishing house did all of the publicity and marketing work. That all changed while I was at the firm. Blogging became a thing. Interactive websites became important. These days, six years later, I spend three-quarters of my time doing publicity and marketing. (Or, at least, it feels that way!) But even then, when marketing demands were much lighter, they were still causing friction with my law career. I tried to go on an abbreviated book tour—two local cities over a weekend—but the minute I got on the train my Blackberry started buzzing. So, between the increasing friction, and the fact that my contracts were starting to provide a legitimate living, it made sense to focus exclusively on writing. My partner mentor, right after I started, asked me, jokingly, "Why are you here? If someone would pay me to write something other than briefs I wouldn't be here." So when I left the general attitude was, yay, you! Why did it take you so long?

So, finally down from three careers to one?

Well, it was still one career plus the dissertation for a while. Even at that point—after leaving the firm and embarking on a full-time fiction writing career—I still thought I'd finish the dissertation. My mantra was always, if I get far enough ahead on my writing schedule with the things people are paying me to write I'll go back and finish the PhD. But my writing schedule kept ratcheting up. I was on a book-a-year schedule in law school and at the firm, and then I signed up for three more books at six months apiece. I think it was a year or so after I left the firm that someone published a book that was basically my dissertation topic. I remember seeing that title in the table of contents in the *Journal of British Studies*—and it felt like a blow. It was definitely a nail-in-the-coffin moment. I realized, in a way that I hadn't before, that the dissertation was over. It was a funny feeling, because I had held on to the prospect of finishing the PhD all those years. There was always the nagging sense of something incomplete. There was some shame in having invested all that time, but not having the degree to show for it. And even though the topic had been difficult to research, it was still something that I found engaging and intriguing. I had all my notes. I had two chapters already written. I was going to go finish it, and I was going to submit. But when I looked at that table of contents I realized: it's never going to happen. No. It's entirely over.

Where is your career headed these days?

Right now it's the Wild West in publishing, and no one really knows what's going to happen or where things are going to land. With the advent of e-books and self-publication, the publishing world has changed seismically over the past five years as publishers have scrambled to keep pace, and my career has definitely changed along with it, and continues to change and adapt. I've doubled my writing schedule over the past two years, writing hardcovers for one of the Big Five publishers and paperbacks for another—so we'll see how it all goes! Things are still settling. But this is definitely an interesting new era.

Has it been difficult, balancing such a demanding career with family life?

Fortunately, my husband is very supportive of my career, and he's a big fiction reader, so that helps! But things are about to get even busier for me, as I have a little one on the way. I can't even imagine how life will change once she arrives! I'm fortunate to have good writer friends with small children—in fact one of my most prolific writer friends has four kids under the age of 12, and no nanny. I don't think I can be a superwoman like her, but I am hoping that with some help I can keep up my writing schedule, since writing is more than a career for me: it's a vocation. The books were the impetus for going to grad school, and the reason that my career has had this trajectory. So I am really hoping I can maintain my career in the face of a rapidly changing publishing industry, and with the addition to our family. My goal is to still be writing and publishing when I'm 90.

Looking back, is there any wisdom you wish you could impart to your former grad student self?

I think that life happens by accident a lot of the time, and that had I tried to plan it out, it probably wouldn't have worked as well. I stumbled sideways into the things I wanted and that made for a meandering path, but I'm glad I had the journey. And I wouldn't trade those experiences. Ironically, I think law school probably helped me more with getting that first book published than grad school did. I had thought that having academic credentials and PhD-level work in history as a background for writing historical fiction would impress publishers. But, in fact, what they were all impressed by and kept using in the press releases was that I was a law student. It was "Legally Blonde" writes bodice-ripper. Which just goes to show you can never predict any of this.

Join the Conversation

The Unruly PhD

Doubts, Detours, Departures, and Other Success Stories

Rebecca Peabody

Visit www.theunrulyphd.com for resources related to *The Unruly PhD*.

Index

Printed and bound by CPI Group (UK) Ltd, Croydon, CR0 4YY